Putting the World in a Nutshell

Putting the World in a Nutshell

The Art of the Formula Tale

by

SHEILA DAILEY

The H. W. Wilson Company
1994

Library of Congress Cataloging-in-Publication Data

Dailey, Sheila, 1947–
   Putting the world in a nutshell : the art of the formula tale / by
  Sheila Dailey.
     p. cm.
   Includes bibliographical references.
   ISBN 0-8242-0860-9
   1. Storytelling. 2. Tales—Classification. 3. Oral-formulaic
  analysis. I. Title.
  GR72.3.D35 1994
  808.5′43—dc20   94-829

Printed in the United States of America
First Printing

For Jim, who made this book possible by watching baby Bridget many extra hours.

CONTENTS

CHAPTER 1

An Invitation to Discover the Formula Tale

"I want to do storytelling, but I don't have time to learn the stories," is a plaintive cry heard often from librarians, teachers and social service providers who attend my workshops on storytelling. They are touched by the wonder of storytelling and return to work eager to tell the stories that fell so sweet on their ears. How are they to begin? Even if there is support by supervisors for adapting content to include storytelling, there is the problem of time and motivation.

Indeed, the demands of the job make time a scarce commodity and motivation the nemesis of even the most ardent novice. Add to this boiling cauldron the fact that librarians, teachers and others see storytelling as validating many of their professional goals and yet are frustrated in their attempts to use it. What's to be done?

I am convinced that storytelling does not have to be a difficult or prolonged process, and I am hoping to convince you, too. The stories you will find in these pages are each modeled on a pattern that is centuries old. They are called formula tales and have a strong element of playfulness in language and form. Because of the rhythm and repetition characteristic of these stories you will find them easy to remember.

Formula tales are a genre of folk literature in which the story's logic becomes obvious early in the telling. The fun, then, is watching the story reach a satisfying and predictable end. Stories such as "The House That Jack Built" and "The Old Lady Who Swallowed a Fly" are well-known examples of cumulative tales—a type of formula tale.

This is a collection of thirty-eight such stories, each identified as one of nine types of formula stories. The format is such that the

1

stories are easy to find, learn and tell. Each chapter introduces a formula tale, gives several examples of that type, makes suggestions in the story notes on telling them, and where appropriate, gives sources for finding other titles of that type to enable you to do further research if you are inclined.

In every category I have included examples of both classic and lesser-known stories of the type to encourage you to begin with the familiar and work into the less so. You may wonder if the classic stories included here are still appealing to children of today. The answer is yes. My experience has been that, by and large, children of today have not heard these stories. Whether they have or not, though, the stories are called classic because they have a perennial appeal. You can be confident that your listeners will love them.

When using this book you can go through chapter-by-chapter or jump to a chapter that appeals to you and come back to the others later. However you will want to read chapters one and two first for background information. Whether you read this book sequentially or as your interests lead, you will learn the form that makes up each formula tale and will gain insight into the earthy wisdom that underlies these forms.

If you have ever wanted to tell stories but didn't know how to get started, here is an easy way that has worked for me and for those I have taught to be storytellers. Formula tales are always welcome at any gathering where stories are told and seem endlessly adaptable. I invite you to discover their magic for yourself.

Why Tell Stories?

One night an elderly man seated before a fire somewhere in foothills of the Caucasus Mountains near the Caspian Sea turned to the boy beside him who had listened the night through to the men tell stories, and he said, "Now it is your turn to tell one."

"I cannot," the boy said, "I do not know how to begin . . . and I might not remember every word of the story right."

"What difference does that make," said the man, "No two people ever tell any story the same way. Why should they? A story is a letter that comes to us from yesterday. Each one who tells it adds his words to the message and sends it on to tomorrow. So begin."

Still the boy hesitated. "Go on," said the man, "Or you have no right to listen any more. To listen to stories without ever telling one is harvesting grain without sowing seeds; it is picking fruit without pruning the tree."

When the boy heard this, he knew he could hesitate no longer, and so he began, "Once there was and was not . . ." (Papashvily, p. 3ff).

Most beginning storytellers are unsure of themselves as performers. Still the stories must be *told* if we are to hear them; and, if we love to hear stories, then there is something within urging us to tell them. There are a great many reasons to tell stories. One of the very best reasons I can think of is so we can continue to hear them. Like the boy, we sow stories that we might reap them.

Other reasons to tell stories? Here are just a few:

Storytelling celebrates language and culture.

Storytelling creates a sense of shared time and place.

Storytelling is innate to being human—using the heart to feel, the head to think, voice to tell and ears to hear.

Storytelling draws on a person's own living language and experience, thus enriching the listeners' language and experience.

Storytelling recalls for us the wonder of imagining whole worlds in midair as we did as children.

Storytelling can, and often does, teach the listener to enjoy the printed word.

What is Storytelling?

There are many ways to define storytelling—as communication, or as the use of voice and gesture and narrative form to create meaning in a group of two or more, as group playfulness. For me, especially when I was a new teller, storytelling was a very personal expression of what delighted or moved me.

Yet, in spite of the personal nature of the act of telling, my story choices were almost always the folktales, and more often than not the formula tales—a kind of folktale. I was to learn later that I was part of a large group of tellers who love the folktales.

While not all stories told are folktales—many are personal experiences, or created by a single author—most of the stories told in classrooms and libraries are folktales. They are the general favorite of teachers, librarians and others who work with children and family groups because they are easy to learn and contain powerful statements about what it means to be human. The folktales are, as one psychologist put it, the dreams of humankind finding a voice. When we tell folktales, we step into a long tradition of everyday people delighting in tales from yesterday, told today and passed on to tomorrow.

For centuries storytelling was unquestioned as the premier form of communication and entertainment, whether around the hearth or at the king's table. Storytelling was practiced in every culture and ethnic group in the world, and continues to be used today. Yet some think its use has passed away among so-called "civilized peoples." The truth is we need stories more than ever.

Happily, storytelling is seeing a revival across the nation today. There are a great many free-lance storytellers earning income either part or full-time from their storytelling. There are many more thousands of parents, teachers, librarians, youth group leaders, Sunday school teachers, business people and human services practitioners who are using storytelling on a regular basis at work and at home.

The spark for this cultural movement was the National Storytelling Festival, founded in 1973 in Jonesborough, Tennessee. Two years later, the National Association for the Preservation and Perpetuation of Storytelling, NAPPS, was founded to help spearhead this national movement. The organization, now the National Storytelling Association, numbers about 7,800 and its annual festival attracts 7,000 to 9,000 participants. In addition, many hundreds of festivals, workshops and conferences are held at local, state and national levels.

Why all the interest in storytelling in this the age of media blitzes, sound bites and docudramas? Storytelling is one of the essentially human things we can do. It's fun to hear and tell stories. It's interesting and often deeply meaningful. Its lasting value as entertainment and its affirmation of the human condition make it an activity people will respond to on a deep level. In the giant's castle of television and movies, storytelling is the Jack in the Beanstalk who makes off with the golden goose of meaning and value.

What Are Formula Tales?

As a little girl I heard formula tales such as "The Gingerbread Boy" and "The Little Red Hen" but, like most people, I did not know that they were a certain type of folk literature. Later, I learned that formula tale is a term used by folklorists as a means of classifying one of several kinds of folktales and refers to those stories that have a similarity of plot structure.

The idea of classifying folktales by similarity of plot was first introduced in 1910 by Finnish folklorist, Antti Aarne, who devised a catalog of tale types. Later his work was enlarged and translated by Stith Thompson of Indiana University in 1928 and revised again in 1961. In this basic reference work, *The Types of the Folktale*, some 2,499 folktales are given numbers and categorized within five basic divisions of tales: Animal Tales, Ordinary Folktales, Jokes and Anecdotes, Formula Tales, and Unclassified. There is also the classification of smaller elements within the tales—the motifs. These have been classified and indexed by Stith Thompson into a six volume set called the *Motif-Index of Folk-Literature*.

In both the folktale index and the motif index formula tales are a separate category. Stith Thompson in his later book, *The Folktale*, calls the formula tales a special group of stories in which the form is all important:

> "Formula tales contain a minimum of actual narrative. The simple central situation serves as a basis for the working out of a narrative pattern. But the pattern so developed is interesting, not on account of what happens in the story, but on account of the exact form in which the story is narrated" (p. 229).

What distinguishes the formula tale from other folktales is that the essentials of the story are pared down. The internal structure is clear and the premise for the tale is often repeated several times throughout the telling.

Craig Roney, a storyteller and professor of children's literature from Detroit, Michigan, describes formula tales as two-minute stories because they can be so quickly learned. He describes the tales as having a logic which becomes obvious early in the telling and the fun is in watching the story reach a satisfying and predictable end.

Why Tell Formula Tales?

After years of poring over folktale collections and learning them for telling, I have come to recognize and appreciate the very form of the folktales. I found and continue to find them beautiful. Like C. S. Lewis, author of *The Chronicles of Narnia*, I ". . . fell in love with the form itself: its brevity, its severe restraints on description, its flexible traditionalism" (p. 46). And it was the formula tales I liked better than other types of folktales, perhaps because they are more like word sculptures.

After reading even a few of the formula tales it is easy to see that each type has its own characteristic structure which is readily reducible to a simple outline. Yet, when retold they delight as much as more complex tales. The secret of the formula tale is that it can be quickly reduced to its simplest form, memorized, and then retold plain or fancy. With this approach it takes only a few minutes (usually about ten) to learn the structure of the formula tale. The storyteller is then free to embellish at her leisure. Over time, the storyteller can add as much detail to the story as she wishes, and yet the story is always ready for telling.

I first learned to use this technique by accident as a new teller. The very first story I ever told was an ornate and complex short story by that Russian master of many words—Leo Tolstoy. It took me so long to learn and tell the story (and I didn't tell it very well either!) that I was *not* eager to learn another, not if telling stories was going to be so much work.

After a time I got a collection of folktales from the library. Unknowingly, I had borrowed a book that was mostly formula tales. The stories read easily and were learned quickly. In one week I learned to tell "The Little Red Hen," "The Enormous Turnip," and "The Fat Cat"—all formula tales. My repertoire of stories had jumped from one tedious tale to four in just one week! I was thrilled. My local library was thrilled, too, and asked me to come the following week to tell stories.

Even though I was successful in learning these stories I felt I was cheating because they were so easy to learn. Like many people, I had the idea that I had to suffer for my "art." In fact, storytelling is more like learning to bake cookies—anybody can do it and everybody wants one when you're done.

In addition, a common error in thinking about formula tales is that they are only for small children. Probably this idea took hold in recent years because so many of the stories, with their simple, straightforward plots, appeal to the very young. It is important to note that brevity is not an indication of lack of depth. The formula tales are full of a distilled wisdom that is as old as time itself. It matters not if you learn, as small children do, from the Little Red Hen to "do it yourself" and reap the rewards; or whether you learn from "Who's To Say It's Bad Luck?" (p. 115) that each circumstance has a good and a bad aspect, depending on how you perceive it. The formula tales are for everyone, in every season of life.

Since those early days of learning formula tales a few years have passed. I have researched and told a great many other types of stories—and yes, some of them are long and complex. Still, I always come back to these wonderfully spare tales which wait, like Sleeping Beauties, to be awakened with the kiss of my own words. And I always find in them some fresh insight, some new fun.

Defining the Formula Tales

For the purposes of learning about the formula tales there are at least nine different types: the chain, the cumulative, the circle, the endless, the catch, the compound, the question, and two known generally as "air castles" and "good/bad." Each of these has their own characteristic structure which is readily reducible to a simple outline and can be explained as follows:

Chain

A chain story is a series of events sometimes interrelated, sometimes not. Each event usually occurs as a consequence of the preceding event. The chain story is the most basic of all the formula tales and others (cumulative, circle, and good/bad) are based on the chain.

An example of a classic chain would be "The Death of the Louse," a wry tale in which Mr. Louse falls into the soup, Mrs. Louse cries for her husband, which causes the dog to bark, the cart to roll into a tree, the tree to wither, a bird to pluck its feathers; a boy seeing this, breaks his water jar and his father spanks him. In retaliation the boy throws a stone at bird, bird pecks tree, tree shoves cart, cart runs over dog's foot, the dog bites Mrs. Louse's foot, and her screams revive Mr. Louse.

Cumulative

The cumulative tale is the most well-known of the formula tales. It is a chain story with one distinctive feature—*incremental repetition*.

Which is defined as the instance in which each repetition of the refrain builds on the last action. The effect is of a slowly building spiral. The story winds up the spiral as each new element is added, building tension. When the climax is reached all the elements turn around and slide back down, unwinding the story and bringing it to a swift end (*World Folktales*, Clarkson, p. 239). "The Gingerbread Man" is a well-known example of a cumulative chain story, with the final refrain recapitulating the whole story:
"I've run away from a little old woman
"A little old man
"A cow
"A horse
"A barn of threshers
"A field of mowers
"And I can run away from you too, I can!
"Run, run, fast as you can,
"You can't catch me. I'm the Gingerbread Man!" (Haviland, p. 8)
Another version of this tale is "The Sweet Roll or Why Pigs Root in the Ground" (p. 37).

Circle

A circle story is a chain story in which the story line "bends back on itself," creating a circular form. Usually the main character begins by wishing he was bigger, better, or stronger and goes through a number of transformations finally realizing that he is the biggest, best or strongest. A classic picture book, *Once a Mouse* by Marcia Brown (Macmillan, 1961), has a hermit granting the mouse's wish to be greater and still greater. He changes him into a cat, a dog, and then a tiger which tries to kill the hermit, who then changes him back again to a mouse.

Endless

An endless story is meant to be humorous and is constructed in such a way that a specific task must be repeated an indefinite number of times. "Thousands of Ducks" (p. 61), for example, are on their way to market and must be put over a stream one at a time. The teller continues the repetition of the task of boating the ducks until the listener can bear it no longer and calls to stop the story. An endless story is usually no more than a paragraph or two and the main idea can usually be expressed in one or two sentences.

Catch

The catch story is usually one of two types: the unfinished story, also known as a "round," and the jump story. The unfinished story is told in such a way, either by the main character or the teller himself, that it must be repeated again and again, as in "A Dark and Stormy Night," where the captain calls for a story and the first mate tells a story which begins with the captain calling for a story which begins all over again.

The jump story is set up in such a way that at the most exciting point the teller yells "boo" or some other startling words. "The Man with the Golden Arm" is a well-known example, a lurid tale in which a man whose golden arm is dug up returns from the grave to reclaim it. The man calls with each approaching step, "Who's got my golden arm?" Finally when the ghost is at the foot of the bed the teller yells, "Take it," thereby causing the listener to jump from the unexpectedness. "The Teeny-Tiny Bone" (p. 75) is another example.

Compound Triad

The compound triad story is not specifically cited in the folktale or motif indices as a formula tale. However, it is a concept that is in keeping with Thompson's definition cited above which views the story's pattern to be as relevant as what happens in the story.

A simple triad story usually has three main events with the recurrence of threes throughout, or, as is more often the case, a compounding of threes. That is, in the first half there are three events, then a turning point, and three mirroring events in the second half. A famous example of compound triad is the "The Three Little Pigs," in which each builds his house—one of straw, one of sticks and one of brick—and three times the wolf comes to blow them down.

Question

A question story usually has one central dilemma posed, then a question asked. The structure is much like a fable—a minimum of characters and one or two scenes. Discussion may or may not follow. The question story can sometimes be humorous, but is more often meant to be thought provoking. The dilemma tales of the Ashanti peoples of West Africa are excellent examples of this type. The listener is posed a dilemma in which someone must be chosen to be the best friend, the most fearless warrior, and so on. Often there is no right answer, but such stories help the listener gain discernment by the exercise of deliberation and choice. "The Left Over Eye" (p. 101) exemplifies this form.

Another type of question story in which there is only one answer is usually a test of knowledge or cleverness. "King Solomon's Test" (p. 99) is a good example of this, because King Solomon must choose the true lily from the crafted one.

Air Castles

The "air castles" story is often a wry tale that looks at the human trait of counting on a desired outcome without the necessary planning. "Air castles" has its own heading (J2061) in the motif index rather than being listed under formula tales (Z0-Z99). From country to country the form of this type is basically the same. An individual (milkmaid, farmer, hunter, numskull, etc.) finds or receives a desired object (basket of eggs, jar of honey, deer asleep in thicket, etc.) and begins to spin one fantasy after another about the wealth or gain from the sale of the item. In the excitement of anticipation the object is lost (eggs broken, pot spilled, deer awakened) and, for the listener, a lesson gained.

Good/Bad

The good/bad story is a type of chain story classified as "the climax of horrors" story. Meant to be humorous, the tale is in the form of a conversation between two persons, one of whom says alternately, "that's good" and "that's bad." In "Good or Bad?" (p. 114) a pilot flies a plane (that's good) and falls out of his plane (that's bad), with a parachute (that's good) that won't open (that's bad) into a haystack (that's good) that has a pitchfork (that's bad) but he misses the haystack (oopps!). The story culminates in a "climax of horrors," with each response leading to the relating of a still worse event.

CHAPTER 2

Learning to Tell
Formula Tales

My most anxious experiences as a storyteller revolved around learning stories rather than telling them. I worried more about how to learn stories than any other aspect. Was there some kind of inborn talent needed to remember all those stories? If there was, I was sure I didn't have it.

On one occasion I heard South Carolina-based storyteller Jackie Torrence say that she knew over three hundred stories. "See," I said to myself, "if I want to be a *real* storyteller that's what I will have to do." And since there was no way I could learn that many stories I was convinced I would never be a *real* storyteller.

Actually, it is not how many stories you know that makes you a storyteller but how you tell the stories you *do* know. My husband is a college professor who includes storytelling in his teaching of psychology and in conference presentations. By his own admission he has only three stories in his repertoire, but says he uses them over again every semester. As a result, the stories have become highly polished gems and his students often comment that the stories are one of the best parts of his class.

Jay O'Callahan was the first storyteller I ever heard. It was he who introduced me to the art by way of his marvelously created stories. We became friends and began to write occasionally. In one letter I asked him what he thought it meant to be a storyteller. In his return letter he said, "The desire to tell stories is a gift that once recognized must be worked with and developed." In other words, a person is not born to be a storyteller. Storytelling is not the innate gift. The *desire* to tell stories is. If you are reading this book, very likely you have a desire to tell stories. And, if you have the desire to tell stories, it can be developed.

On Learning a Story

The technique I developed for learning stories is simple and is based on trial and error and reading other storytelling how-to books (see suggestions on pp. 21 and 117). There are many approaches to the story. Being a storyteller involves putting your personal stamp on everything, including how you learn your stories. You may already have a system, or you may want to adapt my suggestions to your own way of learning. The important thing is that you develop a method that works for you.

On Learning Formula Stories

The process of learning a formula tale varies only slightly from learning other types of folktales. The advantage of the formula tale is that much of the memory and outlining work is already expressed in the story. The cumulative tale, for example, always has one final routine at the end that contains the basic elements of the story. The jump story (a type of catch tale), as another example, has so much repetition in it that once you have the word phrase you almost have the whole.

As you will see in the following chapters each of the nine types of formula tales has a characteristic form. Oftentimes, the form *is* the story, as in a question and answer format. In addition, some of the stories in this book are so short that they only require simple memorization of the whole. "Pete and Repeat" (p. 64), for example, takes only a few moments to memorize. The focus is on practicing timing and intonation.

Each story or collection of stories in this book contains story notes to help you in your telling by giving background information that will make your understanding of the story, and therefore your telling richer. You will also find suggestions for telling.

The story formula is included but is not meant to be the only way to organize the story information. You may wish to use/organize the material in some other way. Please do. The formulas act as guidelines for learning.

Story Selection

Selecting a story to tell should include three considerations: yourself, your audience and your program needs. First and most importantly, choose a story you like. This may seem too simplistic a point; but, it is not. Choosing a story you personally like means you will tell it with more energy and enthusiasm, and you will have an easier time learning it. Like practicing the piano, if you enjoy playing, it is no problem—but, if it's something you think you *should* do, it can be pure drudgery.

The matter of story selection is something that will give a personal dimension to your art. Read many stories for telling. Read way beyond the pages of this book, and you will find that there are certain stories to which you are drawn. Some you know immediately you will want to learn. Others will pluck you by the sleeve until you finally tell them. Over time, you will see a pattern in your story choices—like tracks in the snow—and you will begin to find your way through story choices with greater ease and confidence.

The second consideration is your audience. You may tell one type of story for a group of five-year-olds and another for a family group of children and adults of varying ages. The stories in this book have a recommended age level, but please don't take that as a final word on the subject. I have told some very "young" stories to adolescents under the guise of having them retell it to their younger siblings. They will listen quite well and enjoy the story themselves, once given permission to be a child again, if only for a while.

Most of the stories in this book work well with a wide range of children and adults. "The Stonecutter," for example, is a story I have told to every audience imaginable, whereas "The Enormous Turnip" works best with eight-year-olds and under or in a family group where the children are invited up to "act out" the story.

The third consideration is the occasion for the story. Many tellers want to have both ready-made stories for any occasion and stories for certain types of programs or events. The best approach is to simply start reading stories, whether in this book or others. A wonderful resource for finding stories is:

Stories: A List of Stories to Tell and Read Aloud
Office of Branch Libraries
The New York Public Library
455 Fifth Avenue
New York, NY 10016
Contact Marilyn Berg Iarusso, editor

Updated in 1990, it is an annotated list and contains those "stories used by librarians and acclaimed by children." The list is by story title, subject, country or ethnic group and program type.

When considering stories that have a strong ethnic or racial element be sensitive to the stereotypes that may appear. Conversely, try to select stories which celebrate racially diverse groups and include information about them in your introduction of the stories.

A Technique for Learning Stories

ROVER is an acrostic, that, when you read the word vertically, represents the first letter of each key concept word read horizontally. Use this master word to help you remember the steps.

Read
Organize
Visualize
Energize
Rehearse

Read

Once you have decided on the story you want to learn, read it over several times. This is an important step, because, while you may have the idea of the story, there are nuances you may have missed. Underline any "color" words, such as verbs and adjectives that describe. Doing so will reveal the story's subtext of sensory information. Since formula tales are very spare, a simple word like "bony" or "red" can help you zero in on the story's subtleties and will help you to visualize the story when you begin to learn it for yourself.

Organize

Organizing your story in some outline form is the first step to-wards making the story truly your own and not someone else's words on a page. There are several ways to organize: outlining, mapping, and simple memorization.

Since the stories in this book are all formula tales and have the formula provided, use that if you find it helpful. Or, develop your own shorthand for the story using one of the techniques above. Some stories, as discussed, don't need an outline. Longer tales like "The Two Sisters" (p. 87) would require some form of outlining, but a short story like "Who Is Mightiest?" (p. 103) is nearly in outline form already.

If you decide to outline, your approach may be the hierarchical system of I, II, III, and A,B,C. Make sure your outline is not too de-tailed or you will feel tied to it and have difficulty remembering all the sub-points. Another way is to simply note the main events of the story as briefly as possible. The goal is to see how brief you can make your outline and still cover the main points of the story.

A special tip in outlining: relate the main points you have outlined to some part of your body, like your hands. By introducing the kin-esthetic sense, you can remember your story better. I often use one hand and reduce the story to five main points. Then I practice ticking the five points off on my hand. Soon I can leave ticking off of the fingers behind and simply remember the story. On a note card I draw a hand with the story points. When I go back to the hand-drawing, it jogs my memory in a way that abstract recall does not.

Yet another way to outline is a more "right brain approach"—draw a picture of the story. The idea is to draw a schematic picture of the whole story, not just a particular scene. Often called mapping, it can be extremely helpful in learning a story quickly. Since the formula tales have form as central to their nature, drawing a schematic dia-gram can be a shortcut to learning a story. Save your story maps on index cards as memory joggers.

Visualize

The dictionary calls visualization the action of forming mental images or pictures that are not actually present to the senses. We visualize all the time. It is a common human activity, like thinking. We may visualize what a long awaited child will be like, or a special vacation. We even visualize things we are afraid of—like speaking in front of a group or a possible car accident. Most of the time we are not aware we are visualizing because it is just out of our conscious awareness. When learning a story you will want to make deliberate use of this ability to imagine things that never happened.

Take your outline and use it to help you go through the events of the story. Imagine that the story is a play on the inner stage of your mind. You are the director, directing the action of the story. See the characters in costume and the stage set with all the amazing paraphernalia of your folktale.

As children, we visualized all the time; adults called it imaginative play. If you have not used your powers of imagination much in recent years you may find yourself a bit rusty at first. Don't worry. You never lose your ability to imagine and even a little practice shows good results.

The best time to visualize is when you are in a relaxed state, just before falling asleep, for example. Since you have *read* the story several times and *outlined* it so that you are familiar with all the basic elements, this next step of *visualizing* should come easily. If visualizing the story feels forced or simply "not fun," it may be because you have selected a story you do not truly like. Remember that you can better visualize those things that have a positive feeling associated with them.

Energize

The very best stories have a kind of energy to them that is difficult to define, but you always know it when you hear it. Once, when I was teaching a university class on storytelling, a student selected "The Three Little Pigs" for her final story critique. I was startled because there could hardly be a more often told story in the English language. The pleasure would have to be in *how* she told the story, since everyone in the audience knew the plot thoroughly. She had a tough audience, too, because the class had developed a good ear for stories.

Nevertheless, this student's telling was wonderful and memorable because she had taken time during her practice to include the sounds, smells and sights. What she had done was to energize this tired old story with things like very convincing wolf-growls and pig-squeals, as well as helping her audience see and feel the different types of houses of straw, sticks, and bricks by using carefully placed "picture" words.

In other words, to energize your story see where you can judiciously add sounds or other sensory impressions. The *hiss* of a tea pot, the deep *bong* of a church bell. Adding these makes the audience enter into the story. Be careful not to overdo it by giving your listeners too much of a good thing, though.

Rehearse

Rehearsing a story means to practice it until you're sure of yourself in front of a group. As every teller has their own way to practice you may want to try some of these and see which works best for you:

- Say the story out loud when you are alone in the car, the bathtub or wherever. Take risks with your voice. Speak louder than you think necessary, or too fast or too slow. Invent sounds to go with what you are describing. You may hear things coming out of your mouth that surprise and please you. I like to try this in the shower because my voice reverberates and I can get a better idea how the story sounds.
- Find an audience of one. Make sure this is a person who appreciates the type of story you are about to tell and ask him to listen without offering suggestions. The reason for this is that well-meaning people often come up with a list of things they think will improve the story. These changes are only their opinion.

  My experience as a teacher of storytelling is that one or two improvements at a time are manageable, but a host of changes is not. Too many "suggestions" make the teller feel that the story is not "any good" and worse, still, that she as a storyteller is not "good."

  The very best thing to do is to watch your listener's face for expressions that tell you how you are doing. If there is interest, laughter in the right place, or evident pleasure, you know the story is working.
- Record your story on a cassette recorder. Some people prefer this above any other means of rehearsing. The advantage is not only to hear intonation and pacing but double check whether you

have remembered all the parts of the story. You can also replay the tape several times as a memorization device.

The disadvantage here is that your rehearsing is not in a real-life setting where you get the feedback of live listeners. If you do use a cassette, make sure that at some point you try your story on a live audience of one or more people. Otherwise your storytelling performance may be flat or flawed.

Jitters About Telling a Story

Finding and learning stories to tell gets easier and easier the more often you do it. However, telling is the heart of the matter. If you have not yet told a story to a group, you are probably wondering how to gently ease into your first story. Or, if you have a few stories under your belt, perhaps you are wondering how to improve your skills.

In either case my suggestion is the same. Create an opportunity for yourself. Commit to telling a story at some event or gathering and make sure you cannot back out. Setting a firm deadline will focus your energies and force you to do what it is you want to do anyway. Once you get your first taste of a storytelling you will be motivated to try again. If you wait until you think you are "really good," chances are you won't do it at all. The reason is that we are usually more critical of our own performance than are others.

Things to Remember When Telling a Story

It is in the telling that your story emerges from its cocoon. All that came before was preparation for the story's emergence. Following is a list of important things to remember for effective telling:

Prepare Your Environment

Give special attention to the physical setting for your storytelling: it can make or break your presentation. Locate a comfortable and relaxed area for telling. Make sure the room is adequately ventilated and that the temperature is comfortable.

Provide chairs for your listeners unless they are very young (2 to 5 years old). It's hard for older children and adults to sit on a hard floor and listen to a presentation that will last 30 minutes or longer. Also, if you will be telling to middle school or older students and expect them to sit on the floor, they will feel they are being treated like small children and resent it. In such a situation your audience is likely to be unreceptive, no matter how good you are.

If possible, arrange the seats in a semicircle, with the chairs gathered around you. Make sure there is no bright artificial or natural light behind you; if there is, the audience will squint throughout your program. The rule of thumb is to anticipate and eliminate as many distractions as possible.

Create an Impression

Seasoned public speakers say that people begin talking even before they begin to speak. By this they mean that the way we walk to the front of a room, the way we stand, and what we do with our hands and eyes create a series of expectations in our listeners.

If you walk confidently to the front with your shoulders back and chin lifted, then smile across the group, making eye contact with some before you begin, you'll build immediate rapport and receptivity with your audience. If some distraction occurs as you're about to speak, don't be afraid to wait, smiling confidently, until the problem is solved or the noise quieted.

Make Eye Contact

Storytelling is an art that tries to create intimacy between teller and audience. Eye contact is the single most effective means of doing that and building rapport with your audience, one person at a time. Using effective eye contact means that as you tell your story, your eyes move about the room, meeting the eyes of your listeners. Gaze at an individual for only a second and then move on. If you fix on one person and speak only in his or her direction, you'll lose your audience. By moving your eyes from person to person, you're telling your listeners that you're speaking directly to each one of them. This communicates an important and powerful nonverbal message.

If you're unaccustomed to looking people in the eyes, practice making eye contact during everyday conversations with small groups of people. If you're telling stories, look at several people near the front. Make sure you're looking at enough people to appear engaged with the group as a whole.

By looking at your audience, you're also getting information about how the story is going. Is someone screwing up his face and cupping his hand to his ear to hear you? If so, project to that spot more. Is most everyone looking back at you? If yes, you have your listeners' interest. Be alert for such signals. Making adjustments as needed will help ensure your success.

Breathe Correctly

Breathe deeply and fully as you prepare to tell. If you don't know how to "belly breathe," try this. Lie on the floor and put a book on your abdomen. Breathe in. The book should rise slightly if you're breathing deeply. If your breathing is shallow, the book will not rise but your chest will.

Practice until you get the knack of breathing fully. Mastering this technique will allow you to talk for long periods without fatigue or loss of voice. It will also help you pace your stories and give you a sense of calm.

Create an Opening and Closing for Your Stories

Develop a comfortable way to begin and end stories. A typical beginning is to introduce the story briefly—giving its title and telling your listeners where it comes from and why you're telling it—and then to say, "And the story goes like this . . ." When you finish, you can say, smiling, "And that's the story of (title)." Catherine Farrell in *Word Weaving*, her guide to storytelling says that, "Stories need a stage, a certain framework in which they can be set aside, that marks their beginning and ending. . . . To signal that we are going to "tell" and not "talk" takes some staging" (p. 20).

Or you can use some of the following traditional beginnings and endings:

Armenian:

(Opening) "Three apples fell from heaven. One for the teller, one for the listener, and one for the one who heeds the tale."

(Closing) "Snip, snap, snout. My tale's told out."

Haitian:

(Begin by inviting the audience to join in a call and response in order to judge their readiness to hear a story) Teller says, "Cric."

Audience calls back, "Crac." If you feel your listeners' response isn't enthusiastic enough, tease them a bit. Suggest that you aren't yet convinced that they really want to hear a story, and try again.

Resources for Learning More About Storytelling

There are a number of classic and new releases on the art of story-telling.

Here are my favorites:

Baker, Augusta and Ellin Greene. *Storytelling: Art and Technique* (R. R. Bowker, 1977). Lots of helpful suggestions on program-ming and story selection.

MacDonald, Margaret Read. *The Storyteller's Start-up Book* (August House, 1993). *Extremely* helpful for the beginning storyteller, with useful bibliographies. Addresses all aspects of the art.

Farrell, Catherine. *Word Weaving: A Guide to Storytelling* (Word Weav-ing, 1987 [Word Weaving, P.O. Box 5646, San Francisco, CA 94101]). A simple, practical booklet for learning and telling.

Livo, Norma J. and Sandra A. Reitz. *Storytelling: Process and Practice* (Libraries Unlimited, 1986). This book is packed with informa-tion about storytelling, including how-to and background re-search.

Maguire, Jack. *Creative Storytelling* (McGraw-Hill, 1985). A conversa-tional tone, with good advice on adding to and inventing in sto-ries.

Ross, Ramon. *Storyteller* (Charles E. Merrill, 1980: Out of print). A lovely book that approaches storytelling from several points of view. Don't miss the chapter on the flannel board as it would be very helpful for many of the stories in this book.

Sawyer, Ruth. *The Way of the Storyteller* (Viking, 1942). A classic, full of story wisdom.

CHAPTER 3

For Want of a Nail
the Kingdom Failed

The Chain Story

For want of a nail a shoe was lost
For want of a shoe a horse was lost
For want of a horse a knight was slain
For want of a knight a king was killed
For want of a king the kingdom failed
All for the want of a nail
—Nursery Rhyme

The simple rhythms of the chain story are an integral part of the English language. Remember Henny Penny who thought the sky was falling? That story and many others like it were heard in nurseries and around peat fires of the British Isles for centuries and continue today. The chain stories resemble how we experience life, even how we remember events—as a sequence.

The chain story's plot is spare and is told without the incremental repetition used in the cumulative tale. Usually one event kicks off the sequence. In *The Folktale* Thompson calls the chain stories "a simple series, verbal or actual" (p. 230). Such a story type doesn't usually contain embellishments since the form itself suggests simple telling.

The chain stories remind us of the deeper realities of life since they are based on the principle of cause and effect; that is, that every action has a reaction, or conversely, every reaction is the result of an action. Such stories as "The House That Jack Built" are not only fun for children to hear but important, too, because they give children the understanding that there are consequences for their actions and that the created world is a great web of interconnected creatures, events and things.

LAZY JACK

Once upon a time there was a boy named Jack who lived with his mother. She made her living by spinning, but Jack was so lazy he would do nothing the whole day long but sit. Which is why the villagers called him Lazy Jack.

One Monday Jack's mother told him that he must find work or she would boot him out of the house. This roused Jack mightily and he went out and hired himself to a farmer for the next day.

On Tuesday he did his work and the farmer paid him a penny. A handsome sum, Jack thought, but as he was coming home he dropped it into a stream.

"You silly boy," said his mother, "You should have put it in your pocket."

"I will certainly do so another time," answered Jack.

On Wednesday he worked for a dairy farmer who paid him with a pitcher of milk. Jack remembered the wise words of his mother and put the pitcher in his pocket. As he walked the milk sloshed about, until it had all spilled out.

"You silly boy, you should have carried it on your head."

"I will certainly do so another time," answered Jack.

On Thursday Jack went to work for a farmer's wife who paid him with a fine slab of butter. Jack was pleased he remembered his mother's words and put the butter on his head. As he walked home in the late afternoon heat the butter began to melt. By the time he had arrived home his hair and clothes were matted with spoilt butter.

"You surely are the silliest boy ever born," Jack's mother complained, "You should have carried it in your hands."

"I will certainly do so another time," answered Jack.

On Friday he worked for a baker who paid him with the only thing he could afford—a feisty, old tomcat. Jack certainly remembered his mother's words and carried the tomcat tightly in his hands. The old cat resented such treatment and scratched Jack's hands and face. When Jack got home his mother put salve on his scratches and told him sternly.

"You silly boy, you should have tied it with a string."

"I will certainly do so another time," answered Jack.

On Saturday he worked for a butcher who paid him with a piece of meat. Eager to please his mother with such a tasty dinner, he did just as she said. He tied that meat with a string and dragged it behind him the whole way home. His mother watched him from the door as he dragged up the dirty piece of meat which was now worthless.

"Jack, you ninny, you should have carried it on your shoulder."

"I will certainly do so another time," answered Jack.

The next day was Sunday and because there was no meat and no money to buy it they had to eat cabbage. On the next Monday Jack went out once more and hired himself to a cattle man, who gave him a donkey for his work. Jack found it hard to hoist that donkey on his shoulders but he did it. As he staggered slowly down the road with the beast braying in protest, he passed the home of a rich man and his only daughter.

The daughter was a beautiful girl who would not speak. Because of this she had never laughed in her whole life. All the doctors said if someone could make her laugh she would be able to speak. Now, it happened that she was sitting at the window as Jack was passing with the donkey on his shoulders. The sight of Jack with a donkey as big as he on his shoulders made her burst out with a great laugh. Immediately her speech returned.

Her father was so overjoyed he married her to Lazy Jack to keep her laughing and talking. Thus was Jack made a rich man who lived in a fine house. Jack's mother lived there with them too in great happiness.

Story Notes

"Lazy Jack" is based on the classic story by the same name from Joseph Jacob's *English Fairy Tales* (1890). Stories of the hapless Jack are a central piece of folk literature. It was folklorist Richard Chase who brought the figure of Jack to national attention in America when he collected and published *The Jack Tales* in the 1940s.

Jack is found in many European cultures. In Russia he is known as Ivan, in England as John or Jack, as Hans in Germany, and often in many other cultures as the guileless but clever third son. Each culture, however, gives to Jack their own flavor. Hans in the story "Hans In Luck" is sublimely indifferent to circumstances, whereas Jack of this story is so ignorant he succeeds.

The *Storytelling Folklore Sourcebook* describes Jack as ". . . honest, straightforward, one who never suspects the tricks and deceptions of others . . . The deliberations and premeditation of Coyote, Fox or Brer Rabbit are absent in Jack—his uninformed state is not feigned— but his quick wit is legend . . . Jack is always the fool who bumbles his way to success" (p. 25).

Children love this story, probably because they themselves have often run an errand for an adult and done it foolishly or badly. When learning this story, attempt to keep the rhythm of the dialogue between Jack and his mother, by using the same words each time (whether those here or your own invention). It is part of the music of the story and you may find your listeners joining in.

Story Formula

Monday / Jack's mother / work / or be kicked out
Tuesday / farmer / penny / dropped
Mother: "Put it in your pocket"
Refrain: "I will certainly do so another time"
Wednesday / dairy farmer / milk / spilled
Mother: "Carry it on your head" / *Refrain*
Thursday / farmer's wife / butter / melted
Mother: "Hold it in your hands" / *Refrain*
Friday / baker / tom cat / scratched
Mother: "Tie it with a string" / *Refrain*
Saturday / butcher / leg of meat / dirty
Mother: "Carry it on your shoulder" / *Refrain*
Sunday-no food except cabbage because Jack is so foolish
Monday / cattle man / donkey / carries on shoulder
Rich man's daughter laughs at the sight / Jack marries

Other Stories

Other Versions:

Lazy Jack (English) by Joseph Jacobs, illustrated by Barry Wilkinson (World, 1970). This is a picture book version of the original story as collected by Jacobs.

"Silly John" from *Noodles, Nitwits and Numskulls* by Maria Leach, p. 28 (Dell, 1961).

Other Stories of Foolish Errands:

"Jack and the King's Girl" from *The Jack Tales* (Houghton, Mifflin, 1943); *Epaminandas and His Auntie* (African-American) by Sara Cone Bryant (Houghton, Mifflin, 1938); or Eve Merriam's *Epaminandas* (Follett, 1968).

"Silly Saburo" (Japanese) from *Japanese Children's Favorite Stories* by Florence Sakade, p. 45 (Tuttle, 1958).

THE GREAT PLOP!

One autumn there were six Rabbits feeding near a lake in a great forest. A large wild apple tree grew on the banks of the lake and its branches hung over the water's edge. The apples had ripened and begun to fall. One large apple fell into the water when the Rabbits weren't looking. It made a loud "Plop!"

Twitching with fear the six Rabbits bolted off, not knowing what the noise could be, but they were sure it was something large and very scary. They ran fast, fast, faster until they saw Raccoon coming down to the lake.

"Hey, you six. Where are you going so all fired fast?"

"The Great Plop is coming after us!!! Run for your life."

Raccoon was startled by the Rabbit's cries and ran without thinking if he was afraid or not. The six Rabbits and Raccoon passed Squirrel, who wanted to know what was all the rushing about.

"The Great Plop is coming," Raccoon yelled over his shoulder. "Run!" Squirrel didn't know what the Great Plop was, but knew that Raccoon was a cautious sort, and if he was afraid, well Squirrel ought to be, too. Squirrel ran with them.

They ran up the hill and down into the valley, yelling "The Great Plop is coming. Run for your lives!" Fox heard it and ran with them. Deer, always a little timid anyway, heard it and ran with them. Brown Bear heard it and ran with them. Finally, Moose and a whole flock of Geese heard the Rabbit's cries and ran with them.

The yelling, chattering, honking and bellowing could be heard all across the forest. Owl was in his roost, sleeping the day away so he could hunt for his food at night. The ruckus reached his ears and woke him up.

"Whooose making all that noise and disturbing my sleep?"

All the animals came to a halt under Owl's perch in the tall birch tree. They looked up at Owl and began their cries again. "The Great Plop is coming! Save yourself. Fly away."

Owl eyed Moose and said, "Why are you running, mighty one of the forest?"

"Because the Great Plop is coming."

"Whooo is the Great Plop?"

"Well, he's, umm, I don't know. Bear told me about it and he should know." Moose lowered his great head.

"Bear, come forward and tell me, please, whoooo is the Great Plop?"

Bear snuffled a little then admitted it was Deer who told him. Deer was quick to admit it was Fox who had told her. Fox, of course, said Squirrel had told him. Finally Owl traced the story back to the six Rabbits.

"Pray tell me, you six, whooooo is the Great Plop?"

"Well, we don't exactly know who the Great Plop is, but we heard a terrible 'plop!' with our own ears. Who else could make such a sound but something big and scary?"

"Take me to the place where you heard it and we shall see what we shall see," Owl said and flew off with the group.

They led Owl to the lake and pointed to the place where they heard the terrible sound. Just then another apple fell from the topmost branches. Plop! When Owl saw that he said, "See, you silly Rabbits. It's only an apple falling from the tree into the lake. You almost started a stampede in the forest, and all for nothing."

The Rabbits and all the other animals were very happy to learn who or rather what, the Great Plop was and thanked Owl for his help.

Owl flew back to his roost and said, "Maybe now I can get some sleep."

Story Notes

This tongue-in-cheek story is loosely based on a Tibetan tale, "Plop!" (Clarkson, p. 233). It is Tale Type 2033: *A Nut Hits the Cock's Head*. Though most of us are familiar with the Henny Penny and Chicken

Licken versions, this story stems from a version in the *Jataka Tales*, a collection of early stories about the Buddha.

Some folklorists feel that the later versions stemmed from "Plop!" but lost the teaching component while adding the rhyming, game-like element. In this way, they feel (and I agree) that the story lost its core meaning about facing and overcoming your fears and became more about "laughing at" rather than "laughing with" the characters. You will find this story best for young children ages 3–8, or family groups with small children.

Story Formula

Six Rabbits hear apple drop into lake (plop!) and fear sound is
    caused by some fearsome creature—the Great Plop!
They run away, warning: Raccoon, Squirrel, Fox, Deer and Moose.
Finally, they wake up Owl.
Owl asks each one in turn until he gets back to the Rabbits. No
    one knows who the Great Plop is.
Owl returns with all to the lake and sees another apple fall.
Mystery solved.

Other Stories

Another Version:

"Plop!" from *I Saw a Rocket Walk a Mile: Nonsense, Tales and Chants from Many Lands* by Carl Withers, p. 123 (Holt, Rinehart and Winston, 1965).

A Variant:

"Henny-Penny" from *English Fairy Tales* by Joseph Jacobs, p. 118 (Penguin Books, 1971). The traditional English version.

HANS IN LUCK

Hans was a young man who had served his master faithfully for seven years. Since his time of service was over, he went to his master to ask for his wages.

"Master, I should like to return to my mother before she grows too old and I should like to take my wages with me."

"You have served me well these seven years, so I will pay you well," the master said. He handed him a huge chunk of gold.

Hans tried to put the gold in his pocket but it would not fit, so he tied it in a handkerchief and carried it on his shoulder. As he walked along, putting one foot in front of another, he saw a handsome rider and horse. Sighing and speaking loud enough to be heard he said "Oh, what a fine thing it is to be upon a horse. Your shoes never wear out and you come to your destination in no time at all."

The rider reigned up his horse and asked Hans why he walked if riding was so fine.

"I must," sighed Hans, "I have this heavy chunk of gold to carry." Hans held the gold up for the gentleman's inspection.

"I would be glad to help you out," said the rider. "Why don't you set yourself upon my horse and I will take up your burden for you."

"You would! Oh, I am the luckiest of men." Hans handed the gold over, leapt onto the saddle and trotted off. A short way down the road the horse was startled and threw Hans to the ground. A farmer driving his cow to market grabbed the horse's bridle before it bolted down the road.

"Thank you so much," said Hans. "If you hadn't come along I might have been trampled by that horse. I certainly will never ride it again. Now your cow is worth having. If I had a cow like that I would walk behind it and have milk, cheese and butter every day that I live."

The farmer eyed the fine looking horse and said, "Why, if I could give you so much pleasure to have my cow I will give it to you in exchange for the horse." The farmer jumped on the horse and rode quickly away.

Hans walked along quietly behind the cow thinking about his good luck of always having food from his cow. As the sun reached midday the heat gave Hans a terrible thirst. He couldn't think what to do as he had no money to stop for a bite to eat. Then he remembered his cow. Hans had no pail so he held his wool cap beneath the cow as he began to milk her. Clumsy at milking, he irritated the cow who gave a swift kick to his head.

As Hans was sitting in the dust rubbing his head a butcher came along the road carrying a young pig in a wheelbarrow. "What's this?" asked the butcher of Hans, who told the whole story. The butcher gave him a drink from his flask and told him, "That old cow would give no milk. Her bag's all dried up. And a poor bit of meat she would make. Because you seem like such a fine young man I will give you this pig in return for the cow. What do you say?"

Hans could not believe his luck. "Surely, I was born under a special star! Now mother and I can have our fill of sausages, bacon, and ham." Off he went pushing the wheelbarrow ahead of him. As he walked he thought how wonderful his life was—whenever anything went wrong, immediately it was set right again.

Before long he met a boy carrying a fat goose under his arm. They said hello and Hans began to tell of all the excellent exchanges he had made, the gold for the horse, the horse for the cow, and the cow for the pig. The boy agreed he had done well.

"Still, my goose is the fattest I have ever seen and I am on my way to a wedding feast to sell it for a good price." Then the boy began to look around suspiciously. "I should tell you that the mayor's pig has been stolen in the town where you are headed. It may be you have traded your horse for the mayor's pig. They'll put you in jail for sure."

Hans was very scared. "What shall I do? Where can I hide with a pig? Will you take the pig in exchange for your goose?"

"As I am going on to the wedding feast in another town it is no great matter whether they feast upon a goose or a pig. I will help you out."

The boy took the wheelbarrow and hurried off and Hans carried the goose under his arm thinking that he got the best of the bargain. He knew that he would not only have a fine roast but a feather pillow to lay his head on. As he walked into the city square he saw a grinder with his wheel set up for sharpening scissors and knives for the townspeople. He was grinding so quickly, his stone whirring so fast that his coat blew out from behind.

"I see that all is well with you, grinder," Hans said with admiration.

"Indeed, what could be better than to be a grinder? Every time I put my hand in my pocket there is the jingle of coins. But where did you buy such a fine goose?"

"I didn't buy it. I traded it for a pig."

"And where did you get the pig?"

"That I got for a cow."

"And the cow?"

"The cow I took in trade for a horse."

"And the horse?"

"Well, that I got in exchange for a lump of gold as big as my head."

"And the gold?"

"It was payment for seven years service."

"I see that you are a man who knows how to take care of himself," said the grinder slyly. "It seems that all you lack is to be able to put your hands in your pocket and hear the jingle of coins. Then your fortune is made."

"Oh yes, but how can I with only a goose to my name?"

"You must be a grinder as I am. It doesn't take much skill. All you need is a wheel like this one. Of course, it's a little worn from use, but you need not give me anything for it but that goose. What do you say?"

"How generous of you! I am the luckiest person on earth. If I will have money whenever I put my hand in my pocket, I don't need to ever worry again." He loaded the stone onto his shoulder and went on, his eyes shining with joy.

Hans had been walking since leaving his master's service at daybreak. He was very hot and tired and hungry. He had no food and no money to buy any and the stone was heavy, heavy, heavy. He thought how nice it would be if he didn't have to carry this stone just then.

Then he saw a well in a farmer's field and managed to get to it. As he set the stone on the edge of the well and started to draw up the bucket of cool water, Hans lost his footing and pushed the stone into the well. It made a great splash.

Hans clapped his hands for joy and thanked God for delivering him from so heavy a load and in such a way that there was no one to blame for the loss of the grinding stone. Now, at last, with a light heart free from every burden, Hans ran on until he was at home with his mother.

Story Notes

"Hans In Luck" is classified as Type 1415: *Lucky Hans*, and is a "swapping story" in which the main character keeps trading down, each exchange being for something of less value. This type of story is well known in Europe, the Middle East, and India. Clarkson tells us in *World Folktales* that the type is especially popular in Scandinavia (p. 79). Hans Christian Andersen, a Dane, retold this story as "What the Good Man Does Is Always Right."

Many tellers see Hans as a fool who doesn't know any better—like Jack in "Lazy Jack"—and tell the story with that particular emphasis. Should we pity poor Hans or does Hans have the right idea after all? His blithe acceptance of all that comes his way, his ability to see the good of a bad bargain, and the "lucky" coincidences that come to his aid at just the right moment make him a strong character. Consider, too, though he has lost material things, he has lost nothing essential. In the end he is restored to his mother as happy as he was at the outset—perhaps happier.

Story Formula

Master / gold / carries on head
Rider / horse / thrown by horse
Farmer / cow / kicked by cow
Butcher / pig / stolen property
Boy / goose / of lesser value
Scissors grinder / grinding stone / drops in well
Happy at last

Other Stories

"The Foolish Man" from *Once There Was and Was Not* by Virginia A. Tashjian, p. 3 (Little, Brown, and Co., 1966). The main character goes in search of fortune and does not recognize it when it comes.

Happy Go Lucky retold and illustrated by William Wiesner (Seabury Press, 1970). This picture book is set in Poland and retells the story with Polish place names.

"Lazy Harry" from *The Complete Grimm's Fairy Tales* (Random House, Inc., 1972). A very tongue-in-cheek telling which combines "Hans In Luck" and "Lazy Jack" except that Harry is already married to one as lazy as he and together they find that less is better.

"Gudbrand on the Hillside" (Norwegian) reprinted in *Best Loved Folktales of the World* selected by Joanna Cole, p. 300 (Doubleday, 1983). A husband sets out to sell a cow and swaps until he has nothing, and his wife says she is happy because he always makes the right decisions.

CHAPTER 4

Winding Up and Winding Down

The Cumulative Tale

There was an old lady who swallowed a cow.
She swallowed the cow to catch the dog.
She swallowed the dog to catch the cat.
She swallowed the cat to catch the bird.
She swallowed the bird to catch the spider.
That wriggled and jiggled and tickled inside her.
She swallowed the spider to catch the fly.
I don't know why she swallowed the fly.
Perhaps she'll die.
—Folk Song

The cumulative tale is the most familiar of the formula tales. It is a chain story with one significantly different feature. It contains *incremental repetition* in which a simple phrase is repeated over and over again, each time with additions. The effect is of a slowly building spiral. The story winds up the spiral as each new element is added, building tension. When the climax is reached all the elements turn around and slide back down unwinding the story and bringing it to a swift end.

Learning a cumulative tale is often as easy as just telling it aloud to yourself because the basic elements are repeated throughout the story, reinforcing learning in the telling. Thompson says of this type of story, "Most of the enjoyment, both in the telling and listening, is in the successful manipulation of the ever-growing rigmarole. The cumulative tale always works up to one final routine containing the entire sequence" (p. 230). The children learn it readily, too. You will find that often children can tell the story after one or two hearings.

The other advantage of this type of story is that by making it participatory and using refrains, listeners will ask for the story again and again.

As a child the cumulative tale "The Gingerbread Boy" was a personal favorite. I would ask for the story of the naughty cookie-boy many times. Then at bath time I would gleefully repeat the rhythmic taunt he called over his shoulder—

"Run! run! as fast as you can.

You can't catch me, I'm the Gingerbread Man!"—

as I tried to escape the inevitable scrubbing. While I was playful with the story parts, I nevertheless heeded the cautionary lesson of the fox who used the Gingerbread Boy's own pride to catch him and eat him.

As you read through the following cumulative stories look for the incremental repetition and listen for the rhythmic repeats. These are the melodies that make the story fun and memorable.

THE FOX'S TAIL

Once there was an old woman coming back from town with a pail of milk. When she had walked part way home, she set the pail of milk down and took a knife from her bundle to cut twigs for her fire. She wasn't looking when a fox sneaked up behind her and drank up all the milk.

The woman was so angry she grabbed the fox's tail and chopped it off.

"Ooowwww," wailed the fox, "please sew my tail in place. A fox without a tail is no fox at all."

"Not until you bring me more milk, you naughty fox."

The fox agreed and set off down the road. In no time at all he came to a cow by the side of the road.

"Cow, Cow, will you give me some milk to give to the old woman so she will sew my tail in place?"

The cow chewed slowly and said, "Not until you bring me some grass."

"Oh, bother," said the fox and went on down the road until he came to a field.

"Field, Field, will you give me some grass to give to the cow to get some milk to give to the old woman so she will sew my tail in place?"

The field rustled softly, "Not until you bring me some water."

"Now it's water, is it," muttered the fox and went on down the road until he came to a river.

"River, River, will you give me some water to give to the field to get some grass to give to the cow to get some milk to give to the old woman so she will sew my tail in place?"

The river slithered over the rocks, "Not until you bring me a jug."

"A jug! What next?" He went on down the road until he came to a young girl, sitting with her basket for market.

"Girl, Girl, will you give me a jug to give to the river to get the water to give to the field to get the grass to give to the cow to get some milk to give to the old woman so she will sew my tail in place?"

The girl laughed a silky laugh, "Not until you bring me a blue bead for my necklace."

"Ohhh, where shall I find a blue bead?" He went off down the road until he came to a peddler.

"Peddler, Peddler, will give me a blue bead to give to the girl to get the jug to give to the river to get the water to give to the field to get the grass to give to the cow to get the milk to give to the old woman so she will sew my tail in place?"

The peddler grumbled, "Blue beads are not for free. It will cost you one egg."

"One egg, is there no end to the things I must do?" He went off down the road until he came to a chicken.

"Chicken, Chicken, will you give me an egg to give to the peddler to get the blue bead to give to the girl to get the jug to give to the river to get the water to give to the field to get the grass to give to the cow to get some milk to give to the old woman so she will sew my tail in place?"

The chicken clucked and scratched, "Bring me some grain, *bawk*, bring me some grain."

"Now it's grain. I shall never get my tail sewed on." The fox felt sorry he had ever stolen the milk. He went on down the road until he came to a miller who grinds grain in his mill. The miller had sacks and sacks of grain.

"Will you give me some grain to give to the chicken to get the egg to give to the peddler to get the blue bead to give to the girl to get the jug to give to the river to get the water to give to the field to get the grass to give to the cow to get some milk to give to the old woman so she will sew my tail in place?"

And the miller said yes.

Quick as a wink the fox took the grain to the chicken and the chicken gave him an egg. He took the egg to the peddler and the peddler gave him a blue bead. He took the blue bead to the girl and the girl gave him a jug. He took the jug to the river and the river gave him water. He took the water to the field and the field gave him grass. He took the grass to the cow and the cow gave him milk.

When it was all done he took the milk to the old woman and she sewed his tail in place.

Story Notes

Adapted from Thompson's Type 2034: *How the Mouse Regained Its Tail* and Nonny Horgrogian's Caldecott Winning book, *One Fine Day* (Macmillan, 1971).

This story can be handy for getting the attention of a restless audience. A number of years ago, I was doing a program for an elementary school. The hour was up, but the principal asked me to keep the children a bit longer because of traffic in the hallway. "Just tell a couple minutes worth," he said. Now that's an interesting statement to a storyteller, since I didn't have any two or three minute stories. Then I remembered "The Fox's Tail." I usually told it as a longer tale with lots of group participation. On this occasion, I told it without the participation and as rapidly as possible to keep it within the time limit. The result was a tongue tangling, lickity-split repetition of the cumulative refrain. The kids roared their approval!

Since then, I've added a game element. I ask the audience to time me and see if I tell it in under three minutes. This added dimension of making a game of the story works wonders for settling fidgety listeners.

Story Formula

Fox sees milk and drinks, old woman cuts tail, fox asks to have it
   sewn back on, woman demands more milk in return
Cow demands grass
Field demands water
River demands jug
Girl demands blue bead

Peddler demands egg

Chicken demands grain

Miller gives grain

Final formula: miller gives grain, chicken gives egg, peddler gives
    bead, girl gives jug, river gives water, field gives grass, cow gives
    milk, old woman sews tail

Other Stories

The Old Woman and Her Pig by Paul Galdone (McGraw Hill, 1960).
    Galdone's picture-book retelling of Joseph Jacobs classic.
The Monkey's Whiskers by Anne Rockwell (Parent's Magazine Press,
    1971). A picture-book version of the "cat and mouse" motif. This
    book is out-of-print but available in most library collections.
"The Cat and the Mouse" from *Tales of Laughter* by Kate Wiggen
    (Doubleday and Company, 1926) or reprinted in *World Folktales*
    by Atelia Clarkson and Gilbert B. Cross, p. 237. (Scribner's Sons,
    1980). Essentially the same story only with a cat and mouse.
    Wiggen's charming retelling uses a musical refrain: "First she
    leapt, then she ran, till she came to the (next item in sequence),
    and thus began:"

THE SWEET ROLL OR WHY PIGS ROOT IN THE GROUND

Once there was a man and a woman who had lived many years together in a little house in the woods. One day the old man said to the
old woman: "Grandmother, I am hungry for your tasty sweet rolls.
Make me one, please?"

"What will I make it with? We have no flour. Not one bit."

"Scrape it from the floor if you must, but *please* make me one of
your sweet rolls."

The old woman wanted to oblige so she took a whisk broom,
scraped the bottom of the cupboard and swept the bottom of the flour
bin. When she had gathered about two handfuls of flour, the old
woman added sweet cream and sugar, patted it into a round bun and
fried it in butter. When it was brown and crusty, she put it in a tin
plate on the windowsill to cool.

The sweet roll sat there, then suddenly quivered and shook. It hopped off of the tin plate and onto the floor. Past the old woman, it rolled out the door, onto the porch and across the yard, past the old man standing guard. On and on it rolled, away from the wood as fast as it could, until at last it met a rabbit.

"Sweet roll, sweet roll, what a tasty morsel you seem.

I'll eat you up, all sugar and cream."

The sweet roll laughed, "Don't eat me, please, Mr. Long Ears, and I'll sing you a song:

> *I was scraped from the cupboard*
> *Swept from the bin*
> *Fried in butter*
> *And set in a tin*
> *I've run from the old woman*
> *I've run from the old man*
> *And I'll run from you*

Before the rabbit had time to blink the sweet roll rolled away. On and on it rolled, past blue rivers and meadows of gold, until it met a wolf, who said,

"Sweet roll, sweet roll, what a tasty morsel you seem.

I'll eat you up, all sugar and cream."

The sweet roll laughed, "Don't eat me, please, Mr. Big Teeth, and I'll sing you a song:

> *I was scraped from the cupboard*
> *Swept from the bin*
> *Fried in butter*
> *And set in a tin*
> *I've run from the old woman*
> *I've run from the old man*
> *I've run from the rabbit*
> *And I'll run from you*

Before the wolf could think twice the sweet roll was gone. It rolled on and on until it came to a bear. The bear took one look at the sweet roll and said:

"Sweet roll, sweet roll, how tasty you seem.

I'll eat you up, all sugar and cream."

The sweet roll laughed, "Don't eat me, please, Mr. Big Paws, and I'll sing you a song:

I was scraped from the cupboard
Swept from the bin
Fried in butter
And set in a tin
I've run from the old woman
I've run from the old man
I've run from the rabbit
I've run from the wolf
And I'll run from you

And quick as a wink the sweet roll was gone. On and on it went until it reached a pig. The pig looked at the sweet roll and said:

"Sweet roll, sweet roll, how pretty you seem,
All dressed up in sugar and cream."

The sweet roll was pleased to be thought pretty and sang his song:

I was scraped from the cupboard
Swept from the bin
Fried in butter
And set in a tin
I've run from the old woman
I've run from the old man
I've run from the rabbit
I've run from the wolf
I've run from the bear
And I'll run from you

Now pigs are known to be smart creatures and this one was no exception. The pig put a hoof to his ear and said, "I am getting old and hard of hearing would you come and sit on my snout and sing your pretty little song again?"

The sweet roll sat on the pig's snout and began his song again, when suddenly the pig threw his head back and snapped that sweet roll up—but he only got half. No one knows what happened to the rest, but that pig has been looking for that other half ever since. That's why pigs root in the ground, they are still looking for the other half of the roll.

Story Notes

Most readers will recognize this as a variant of the famous story, "The Gingerbread Man." After reading many versions, I created this story. The rhymes are original. Like all cumulative stories it has a final routine, followed by the climax, but the addition of the twist, of making it a "why" story in which we learn why pigs root in the ground, adds a new dimension.

This story type is known as "the fleeing pancake." Many versions make the runaway either a bun (Russian), gingerbread (American) or johnnycake (English). When learning this story be aware that the early details of *how* the flour is gathered become part of the refrain so you will need to include it. However, if you choose, you don't have to memorize the refrain.

When telling this story for young children, give them encouragement to join in the refrain. Sometimes the children will join in spontaneously or if you gesture to them they will know to join you. It isn't necessary to memorize the internal rhymes in the story, such as ". . . across the floor and out the door," but the story has so much rhythmn that you may find that the rhymes appear in your telling anyway.

One final note: If the story seems too spare of description don't be afraid to add your own. When each animal appears, for example, you can give a short description.

Story Formula

Old woman and old man live in house in the woods

Old woman makes sweet roll which rolls past: rabbit, wolf, bear and pig

Roll escapes each one until he comes to pig who feigns deafness, so roll sits on his snout

Pig eats half—is still looking for the rest

Other Stories

Other Versions:

"The Gingerbread Boy" by Sara Cone Bryant, from *The Fairy Tale Treasury*, selected by Virginia Haviland (Yearling Books, 1972), and in other collections and in picture book format. All about the perils of running away when you're made of gingerbread.

"The Bun" from *Russian Fairy Tales* collected by Aleksander Afanàs'ev, p. 447 (Parthenon Books, 1945). This version is closest to my own but has bun meet a rabbit, wolf, bear, and fox.

"Journey Cake Ho" by Ruth Sawyer (Viking, 1956). Illustrated by Robert McCloskey, this story resembles the English version. Sawyer's strong storytelling voice can be heard in the text.

"Johnny-Cake" from *English Fairy Tales* by Joseph Jacobs, p. 162 (Puffin Books, 1972). In this classic English version the cake escapes from a young boy and meets its end with the fox.

THE ENORMOUS TURNIP

Once upon a time grandfather found a turnip seed. He went to his garden, dug a hole and put the seed in. As he covered the seed with dark earth, he sang, "Grow sweet, grow strong, grow big."

That turnip surely did grow. It grew and grew and grew until it was enormous.

When the turnip was as big as it could get, Grandfather decided to pull it up and make turnip soup. He pulled and he pulled and he pulled, but he couldn't get it out. He called Grandmother to help. Grandmother pulled on grandfather. Grandfather pulled on the turnip. He pulled and he pulled and he pulled, but he couldn't get it out.

So, Grandmother called her grandson. The grandson pulled on the grandmother. Grandmother pulled on grandfather. Grandfather pulled on the turnip. He pulled and he pulled and he pulled, but he couldn't get it out.

So, the grandson called the dog to help. The dog pulled on the grandson. The grandson pulled on Grandmother. Grandmother pulled on Grandfather. Grandfather pulled on the turnip. He pulled and he pulled and he pulled, but he couldn't get it out.

So, the dog called the cat to help. The cat pulled on the dog. The dog pulled on the grandson. The grandson pulled on Grandmother. Grandmother pulled on Grandfather. Grandfather pulled on the turnip. He pulled and he pulled and he pulled, but he couldn't get it out.

So, the cat called the mouse to help. The mouse pulled on the cat. The cat pulled on the dog. The dog pulled on the grandson. The grandson pulled on Grandmother. Grandmother pulled on Grandfather. Grandfather pulled on the turnip. He pulled and he pulled and he pulled and *kerplop,* up came the turnip. And Grandfather said, "At last we can have turnip soup."

Story Notes

Versions of this well-known story can be found in many collections and picture books. Most resemble each other very closely. My version is based on "The Turnip" from *Russian Fairy Tales* (Guteman). It has a motif number of Z49.9. Though the chain of interdependent members with the least being the most important is a common one, there are no real variants for this story.

When I tell this story I ask children to come from the audience and help me. I choose Grandfather first, then as each new character comes up in the story I add them (rather than bringing up all the characters at once). The audience joins in on the refrain, "And they pulled and they pulled . . ." It is a story that works well for small and large groups.

I have often asked the audience to suggest who we might add after the mouse. In this way I invite the children into story creation. On one occasion I let the children invent the chain extension until we reached the atom!

Story Formula

Turnip / grandfather / grandmother / grandson / dog / cat / mouse
Final formula: mouse pulls on cat, cat pulls on dog, dog pulls on
    grandson, grandson pulls on grandmother, grandmother pulls on
    grandfather and grandfather pulls on the turnip

Other Stories

Other Versions:

The Great Big Enormous Turnip by Alexei Tolstoy, illustrated by Helen
    Oxenbury (Watts, 1968).
"The Turnip" from *I Saw a Rocket Walk a Mile: Nonsense, Tales and
    Chants from Many Lands* by Carl Withers, p. 98 (Holt, Rinehart
    and Winston, 1965).

THE FAT CAT

Once a woman lived in a house with only her cat to keep her company. One day the old woman decided to make a pot of soup, but she had
no salt. She turned to the cat curled up by the fire and said, "Little
Cat, will you watch my soup while I go the store?"

"Yes, indeed," purred Cat.

The old woman went to the store. As soon as she was gone the cat
hopped up on the stove and ate the soup (*gulp, slurp, slurp*) and the pot
(*gulp, slurp, slurp*).

Just then the old woman came home and saw the cat.

"Little Cat, how did you get so fat?"

The cat said, "I ate the soup, I ate the pot and now I am going to eat
YOU (*gulp, slurp, slurp*)." You can imagine what a full stomach that
gave him, even so, he was still hungry.

So the cat went walking down the road and who should he see but
a neighbor, Mr. Skolinkinlot, out for a stroll. Mr. Skolinkinlot took
one look at the cat and said, "Little Cat, how did you get so fat?"

The cat said, "I ate the soup, I ate the pot, I ate the old woman and
now I am going to eat YOU (*gulp, slurp, slurp*)." And the cat got bigger,
but he was still hungry.

So the cat went walking down the road and who should he see but
another neighbor, Mr. Skohotintot, weeding in his garden. Mr.
Skohotintot wondered at a cat so large and said, "Little Cat, how did
you get so fat?"

"I ate the soup, I ate the pot, I ate the old woman, I ate Mr.
Skolinkinlot and now I am gong to eat YOU (*gulp, slurp, slurp*)." And
the cat got bigger, but he was still hungry.

So the cat went walking down the road and who should he see but five birds prancing about. They took one look at the cat and said, "Little Cat, how did you get so fat?"

"I ate the soup, I ate the pot, I ate the old woman, I ate Mr. Skolinkinlot, I ate Mr. Skohotintot and now I am going to eat YOU (*gulp, slurp, slurp*)." And he gobbled up every one of those birds, but he was still hungry.

So the cat went walking down the road and who should he see but seven girls dancing. They stopped their dancing and spinning, took one look at the cat and said, "Little Cat, how did you get so fat?"

"I ate the soup, I ate the pot, I ate the old woman, I ate Mr. Skolinkinlot, I ate Mr. Skohotintot, I ate five birds prancing and now I am going to eat YOU (*gulp, slurp, slurp*)." And he gobbled up those dancing girls, slippers and all. By now the cat was enormous, but he was still hungry.

So the cat went walking down the road and who should he see but a little boy with a wooden toy. The little boy did not see the cat until he was nearly on top of him. The little boy's eyes almost popped out of his head and he said, "Little Cat, how did you get soooo fat?"

"I ate the soup, I ate the pot, I ate the old woman, I ate Mr. Skolinkinlot, I ate Mr. Skohotintot, I ate five birds prancing, I ate seven girls dancing and now I am going to eat YOU (*gulp, slurp, slurp*)." And he ate up the little boy and his wooden toy and got bigger, but he was still hungry.

So the cat went walking down the road and who should he see but an old man with a tin can. Why the old man had a tin can no one knows, but when he saw the cat he rubbed his eyes to make sure it was really true. "Little Cat, how did you get so fat?"

"I ate the soup, I ate the pot, I ate the old woman, I ate Mr. Skolinkinlot, I ate Mr. Skohotintot, I ate five birds prancing, I ate seven girls dancing, I ate a little boy with a wooden toy and now I am going to eat YOU (*gulp, slurp, slurp*)." And he ate up the old man and his tin can. By now the cat was truly enormous, but he was still hungry.

So the cat went walking down the road and who should he see but the woodcutter Mighty Max with his giant ax. Mighty Max thought the cat was the biggest he'd ever seen, "Little Cat, how did you get so fat?"

"I ate the soup, I ate the pot, I ate the old woman, I ate Mr. Skolinkinlot, I ate Mr. Skohotintot, I ate five birds prancing, I ate seven girls dancing, I ate a little boy with a wooden toy, I ate an old man with a tin can and now I am going to eat YOU."

"Think again my little friend!" He took his ax and cut open the fat cat. Out came the old man with his tin can

and the little boy with his wooden toy

and the seven girls dancing

and the five birds prancing

and Mr. Skohotintot

and Mr. Skolinkinlot

and the old woman

The old woman took her pot full of soup *and* her cat home with her. She sewed up the cat's stomach. Then the cat curled up by the fire and never did eat soup ever again.

Story Notes

The story of the cat swallowing extraordinary or impossible things is a cumulative tale known worldwide. Thompson gives it a Tale Type number 2027: *The Fat Cat*, indicating its frequent recurrence in this form.

This story is adapted from Jack Kent's *The Fat Cat—A Danish Folktale* (Scholastic Books, 1971). Most of the repetitive speech and rhyme as well as a few extra characters are my additions. The children love this story because it lends itself so well to joining in. When I tell it, I encourage listeners to say the refrain, "Little Cat how did you get so fat?" and the refrain that lists those swallowed, "I ate the soup, I ate the pot, I ate the old woman, etc., etc."

A Scandinavian version of the story is told of a fat troll or a fat wolf. The formula is as follows: wolf/troll eats master / wife / servant / daughter / son / dog / cat. When the wolf/troll comes to the cat, the cat scratches him open and rescues all the victims.

Story Formula

Cat eats: old woman / Mr. Skolinkinlot / Mr. Skohotintot / five
birds prancing / seven girls dancing / a little boy with a wooden
toy / an old man with a tin can / Mighty Max and his giant ax
Final formula: "*I* ate the soup, I ate the pot, I ate the old woman, I

ate Mr. Skolinkinlot, I ate Mr. Skohotintot, I ate five birds prancing, I ate seven girls dancing, I ate a little boy with a wooden toy, I ate an old man with a tin can and how I am going to eat YOU."

Other Stories

Other Versions:

Norwegian Folk Tales by Peter C. Asbjørnsen and Jørgen Moe (Viking, 1960).
Tales of Laughter: A Third Fairy Book by Kate Wiggen (Doubleday, 1954).

Other "swallowing stories":

"Drakestail" from *Favorite Fairy Tales Told in France* retold by Virginia Haviland, illustrated by Roger Duvoisin, p. 76 (Little, Brown and Company, 1959). This famous French tale is a chain story which has Drake going to the King to get his money back. On the way he swallows friend fox, ladder, river, and wasp's nest—all of which become necessary.
The Wolf and the Seven Little Kids translated by Anne Rogers, illustrated by Otto S. Svend (Larousse, 1977). This story comes from the Grimm Brothers' collection. The wolf swallows seven baby goats, the mother goat finds the sleeping wolf and cuts him open, replacing kids for stones, causing the wolf to drown.
"The Cat and the Parrot" from *World Folktales* by Atelia Clarkson and Gilbert B. Cross, p. 224 (Scribner's Sons, 1980). A cumulative tale in which the cat eats her host's food and then her host. Still not satisfied she eats an old woman, a man and a donkey, a king, a queen, an entire wedding party, and two land crabs who cut her open.

ROOSTER GOES TO THE BALL

A ball was held for all the birds and handsome Rooster was invited to go. He cleaned his feathers until they sparkled, then set out for the ball. On the way he saw a ripe tomato. He quickly ate the tasty fruit, but got his bill all dirty.

What was he to do? He walked on until he came to some Grass.

"Grass," he asked, "please clean my bill for me because I am going to the ball tonight."

"I won't do it," said Grass.

Embarrassed at how he looked, Rooster walked on until he met a Cow.

"Cow," he pleaded, "will you eat Grass, who won't clean my bill, so I can go to the ball tonight?"

"I won't do it," said Cow.

Rooster trudged on until he came to a Stick.

"Stick," he begged, "please will you beat Cow who won't eat Grass who won't clean my bill, so I can go to the ball tonight?"

"I won't do it," said Stick.

Rooster went on until he came to a River.

"River will you rot Stick, who won't beat Cow, who won't eat Grass, who won't clean my bill, so I can go to the ball tonight?"

"I won't do it," said River.

Not knowing what to do he walked on until he met the Sun shining on the path.

"Sun will you dry up River, who won't rot Stick, who won't beat Cow, who won't eat Grass, who won't clean my bill, so I can go to the ball tonight?"

"Certainly I will," said Sun.

So Sun began to dry up River and River began to rot Stick and Stick began to beat Cow and Cow began to eat Grass and Grass yelled, "Stop eating me. I'll clean Rooster's bill."

At last, when Rooster's bill was clean he went to the ball and danced all night.

Story Notes

"Rooster Goes to the Ball" is adapted from "The Heron's Ball" (Withers, p. 53). I include it because it is an interesting variation on "The Fox's Tail." Unlike Fox, Rooster cannot get willing helpers and must eventually go to the boss—the Sun—to convince the others. Some may find the tone of the story too negative. I did not find it so. In fact,

I think this wry story resembles an aspect of everyday life that most have experienced, even children. This story would be good in any setting or in a program on being helpful.

Story Formula

Rooster tries to clean his bill
Grass won't clean bill
Cow won't eat Grass
Stick won't beat Cow
River won't rot Stick
Sun dries up River
Final formula: Sun dried up River and River rotted Stick and Stick beat Cow and Cow ate Grass and Grass yelled, "Stop eating me. I'll clean Rooster's bill."

Other Stories

Other Versions:

"The Old Woman and Her Pig" from *English Fairy Tales* by Joseph Jacobs, p. 18 (Puffin Books, 1972). Or *The Old Woman and Her Pig* by Paul Galdone (McGraw Hill, 1960). A classic in folk literature, this cumulative chain is a variant of "Rooster Goes to the Ball."
"The Wee, Wee Mannie" (Scottish) from *Best Loved Folktales of the World* selected by Joanna Cole, p. 281 (Doubleday, 1983). Found in many collections and picture-book versions. The humor relies on the Scottish dialect. Unless you are good with dialects, this one is best read aloud.

Another Cumulative Tale:

Bringing the Rain to Kapiti Plain: A Nandi Tale by Verna Ardema (Dial Books, 1977). This rhythmic poem in picture book format, emphasizes the importance of everyone in the chain of events. One of the very few books I recommend memorizing word-for-word or to read aloud.

CHAPTER 5

What Goes Around Comes Around

The Circle Story

> *The wheel is come full circle.*
> —William Shakespeare, *King Lear*

The circle story is one of my favorite types of the formula tales. Although it is a chain story, its unique characteristic is that the story ends where it began, yet all is changed—or is it? That is often the question the listener is left to ponder.

The circle story can be quite eloquent, is often about such important human themes as love and marriage, self-worth, personal responsibility or the nature of our relationship to the divine. Yet the story unfolds in a simple, homely manner. The symbolic meaning of the circle is unity and wholeness. The movement and shape of the story is towards this wholeness. Each of these stories begins with the main character having a fragmentary understanding of a situation, and ends with the restoration of wholeness and a wider view.

Each story included here is similar in form yet very different in meaning. "The Stonecutter," "The Mouse Bride," and "God Is the Strongest" all use similar motifs of sun, wind, cloud, mountain, mouse, and cat, or man to represent orders of being. I deliberately chose them in this way to demonstrate that though the form may be similar, the theme is very different. It is an extremely versatile story form and can be used with many different audiences. Also, depending on how you tell these stories, listeners will see them as either humorous or serious, thus underscoring their universal quality.

ONCE A STONECUTTER

Once a stonecutter worked in a rock quarry at the foot of a high mountain. Each day he would come to the quarry with his hammer and chisel. Each day he would cut stone (*chink, chink, chink*) until exhausted. Each day he would mutter, "I hate this dirty work. I am meant for greater things."

One day he looked up from his work and saw a prince riding by on a chestnut-brown horse. The prince wore a green silk tunic, soft leather pants, and a golden sword hung at his side. The stonecutter watched him pass by and wished with all his soul that he might be like the prince.

"Ah, me, ah, me, if only a prince I could be."

Whether on account of some magic or what, I cannot say, but because he wished it, he became it. He was a prince, galloping down the road on a chestnut-brown horse, wearing a green silk tunic and a golden sword. His heart swelled with pride.

"Now people will look up to me. Now I am fulfilling my destiny."

Suddenly, from the other direction came two white horses pulling a chariot trimmed in gold. The horses drove on so fast the prince had to pull his horse off to the side of the road or be trampled. As the chariot passed by, the prince could see seated within a king with the golden crown of rule on his head.

"What good is it to be a prince," he muttered, "if I must tremble before a king. Being a prince is nothing. There is one greater still."

"Ah, me, ah, me, if only a king I could be."

Because he wished it, he became it. He was a king riding in a golden chariot. The chariot rode on until it passed through the gates of a castle larger and more beautiful than any he could have imagined. He was rich beyond all measure.

He lived many days as a king until one day, as he walked through his garden, a hot sun beat down on his head. Turning to a servant, he growled, "Bring me an umbrella. The sun grows too hot for my head."

As the servant scurried away, the king began to think. There is one greater than I that makes me put something over my head. The thought would not leave him until finally he said,

"Ah, me, ah, me, if only the sun I could be."

Because he wished it, he became it. He was the sun shining in the wide, blue sky. But, he shone down on the land so furiously that the crops shriveled and the rivers dried up. Pleased with his power he cried, "Now I am the greatest of all. No one is greater."

Even as he spoke a small dark rain cloud formed on the horizon. It grew larger and larger until it completely covered the sun.

"What good is it to be the sun if there's one yet greater than I that blocks out my rays."

"Ah, me, ah, me, if only a rain cloud I could be."

Because he wished it, he became it. He was a dark, thunderous rain cloud filling the sky with rain. He rained and rained until the rivers filled up and flooded their banks, destroying the crops.

But there was one unharmed by that rain cloud. It was a great mountain. The rain cloud moved furiously over the mountain, raining thunder and lightening and hail. The mountain was unmoved.

"What good is it to be a rain cloud. There is one still greater than I."

"Ah, me, ah, me, if only a mountain I could be."

Because he wished it, he became it. He was a huge mountain. His foothills spread across the earth, his peaks reached to the sky.

"Now I am the greatest of all. I am unmovable."

As he said these words he heard a sound coming from the base of the mountain (*chink, chink, chink*). It was the sound of a stonecutter cutting away the mountain little by little. He knew at last who was the greatest of all and he wished with all his soul.

"Ah, me, ah, me, if only a stonecutter I could be."

Because he wished it, he became it.

Story Notes

This story was one of the earliest I learned. It should not be surprising that I would learn a story about self-worth when I was just beginning to gain self-esteem as a storyteller. I found it very simple to learn: Stonecutter, prince, king, sun, cloud, wind, mountain, stonecutter. I have used this story in more situations than any other, from a gathering of the local Rotary Club to a support group for clinically depressed persons—and everything in-between. I also use it when I teach others to tell stories. It works wonderfully.

Sources for developing this story were *The Stonecutter* by Gerald McDermott (Viking, 1979) and "Hafiz, the Stonecutter" from the classic storytelling book *The Art of the Storyteller* (Shedlock, p. 179).

Story Formula

Stonecutter becomes prince becomes king becomes sun becomes
rain cloud becomes mountain becomes stonecutter.

Other Stories

Another Version:

The Greatest of All by Eric Kimmel, illustrated by Giora Carmi (Holiday House, 1991). Father Mouse does not learn his lesson as did
the stonecutter.

Other Circle Stories:

Why Mosquitoes Buzz in People's Ears (African) by Verna Aardema
(Dial Books for Young Readers, 1975). A lovely story of consequences in which the reader discovers why Mother Owl won't
wake the sun so that day can come.
Once a Mouse (Indian) by Marcia Brown (Macmillan, 1961). A hermit
grants the mouse's wish to be greater and still greater until his
pride gets him into trouble.
The Mountains of Tibet (Tibetan) by Mordecai Gerstein (Harper and
Row, 1987). A transformation story in which a young boy dreams
of what he shall become.

OTTER'S REVENGE

One day Otter came to King Solomon, demanding justice because
Weasel had killed her young whelps.

"Death to the slayer," wailed Otter. Solomon inquired of Weasel
how this tragedy had happened.

"I cannot be blamed," said Weasel, "Yes, I trampled her whelps as I
sped to war, but the alarm was sounded by Woodpecker's drumming."

Woodpecker came forward and asked to be excused because he had
only done what was right. After all, had he not seen Scorpion whetting his dagger and preparing for war?

Scorpion would have none of it. "I saw tortoise polishing his armor." Tortoise replied that he was only defending himself because he saw Crab sharpening his sword.

"Do not blame me," said Crab, "I saw Lobster swinging her javelin high over her head."

Lobster came forward to speak for herself. "I did no wrong. I was only defending my children against Otter who had gone down into the waters to devour them. Anyone would have done the same."

Solomon look to Otter. "The Weasel bears no guilt. Your children's lives are on your own head. What one sows, one also reaps."

Story Notes

This story is not so well known as some of the other circle stories. My version is adapted from "Whose Was the Blame?" (Ausubel, p. 70). Though it is a somber subject, eight-to-twelve-year-olds like it because they understand very well a discussion on who is to blame for mishaps. It is also a good introductory story for discussing "getting all the facts of a situation."

The ending, in which King Solomon issues the proverb about reaping and sowing, may not be appropriate in every situation. An alternate might be that Otter confesses to her own wrong. Thus softening the moral tone.

I tell several King Solomon stories because I find them not only wise but full of wonder. According to ancient tradition, before Solomon fell from grace, he held dominion over all humans, demons, angels and animals. Legend has it that Solomon could speak the language of animals and birds, that they frequently came to his aid and furnished him with information about the condition of his kingdom.

This story obviously speaks about personal responsibility and/or about the interdependence of life. Another story in this book that has that theme is: "Who Is the Mightiest?" (p. 103)

Story Formula

Otter demands justice because Weasel killed whelps
Weasel / trampled as he sped to war
Woodpecker / drumming for war

Scorpion / whetting his dagger
Tortoise / polishing his shell
Crab / sword
Lobster / swinging her javelin
Otter / tried to eat Lobster's children
Solomon's judgment

Other Story

Who Is the Beast? by Keith Baker (Harcourt, 1990). The theme of the
   rhymed text and art in this picture book is the interconnections
   and similarities among creatures.

THE MOUSE BRIDE

Once there was a family of gray field mice who lived together at the
foot of a high mountain. They had dug a home for themselves in a
rocky crevice where mountain and meadow meet. Each spring more
mouse-children were born and each mouse-child was as gray as the
last.

One warm, spring day a new litter of gray mouse-children was
born and among them a *white* mouse-child. Mother and Father
twitched their tails in wonder and delight. Why should they have
such a special child? After all, were they not the smallest and least of
the creatures that lived in the meadow? Why should such an honor
come to them?

The white mouse-child grew up sleek and swift, along with the
others. Soon it was time for the mouse children to marry and set up
nests for themselves. But what about the white mouse-child? Who
should she marry? Surely, only the mightiest and worthiest husband
would do. Who would that be?

They looked about the meadow. The sun had melted winter snows
away and warmed the earth. All the world had begun to grow again
because of the sun. "The Sun is mightiest, no one but the Sun is
worthy to marry our daughter," Mother and Father said.

Mother and Father set out on the long and dangerous journey to
the top of the misty mountain to ask the Sun to marry their daughter.

The top of the mountain was as close as they dared come to the scorching Sun. Clambering over rocks and around trees, they reached the top.

"Mighty Sun, without you nothing is done. Will you marry our milk-white daughter?"

The sun slid from behind a large cloud.

"Though I am the Sun, I am often undone. The Wind is far stronger. It blows clouds across my face. It knocks down huge oaks and sends animals scurrying for cover. It pushes the rain before it. The Wind is the one to marry your daughter."

The two mice thanked the Sun and wondered how they would find the wind which seemed to be everywhere at once. Suddenly a great gust of wind caught them up and tumbled them nose over tail. In the twitch of a whisker they were staring at wide, dark caves with great boulders heaped on every side.

"These must be the caves of the North Wind," Mother said a little afraid. An eerie, cold wind curled about her. "Who do you seek?" the Wind whistled.

"The mightiest of all to marry our snow-white daughter," Father answered.

The Wind roared. The boulders creaked in their places. "There is one mightier than I. He stands tall and unbroken before my worst storms. He laughs in the face of snow and ice driven by my powerful hand. This Mountain on which you stand is stronger than I. He is the one worthy to marry your daughter."

Mother and Father thanked the Wind and skittered down the face of the mountain until they were standing in their very own meadow. They looked back up the mountain to its great, misty peaks and called out, "Mountain, you are greatest of all, greater than Sun and Wind. Will you marry our snow-white daughter?"

Then Mountain shrugged, "I am a wall to the Wind and a shield to the Sun. It is true I am mightier than they. Even so, I crumble before one I call mightier still."

"Who can that be?" Mother and Father were amazed at such a thought.

"A family of field mice burrowing deep inside me. They nibble away all day until they have made a home for themselves. As the years pass there is less of me and more of them."

Mother and Father shook their tails in wonderment. "Surely this must be a family of *giant* mice." Seeing a burrow they scurried over.

How like their own it was. They sniffed at the door, then hurried in. Inside was a family of gray mice. They discovered that this family had a son who would very much like to marry the snow-white mouse.

"Very nice," said Mother. "Very nice," said Father.

Everyone agreed the marriage of the gray mouse and the white mouse was by far the best match of all. And it was.

Story Notes

"The Mouse Bride" is loosely based on an Ethiopian version "The Marriage of the Mouse" (Courlander, p. 89). Variants of this story are found in India, China, Japan, and I have found it among Native-American stories as well. There are two delightful picture book versions (mentioned in *Other Stories* below) that I like to bring with me when I do a program to show the same story in different cultural contexts.

Story Formula

Gray mouse parents want husband for their white mouse daughter. They ask:

Sun / Wind is greater / blows cloud that covers Sun

Wind / Mountain is greater / resists Wind

Mountain / Mouse is greater / gnaws Mountain

Gray mouse who lives in mountain marries white mouse.

Other Stories

Two Versions from Different Cultures

The Mouse Couple (Hopi) by Ekkehart Malatki (Northland Publishers, 1988). Uses all the Southwestern place names, illustrations of Pueblo life.

The Wedding of the Rat Family (Chinese) Carol Kendall (Macmillan Books, 1988). A very elegant tale and a wry commentary on Chinese upper class life.

GOD IS STRONGER

One year there was a great drought. Ibotity climbed a tree to pray to God for rain when a high wind blew and split the tree. Ibotity fell and broke his leg.

Ibotity wondered at the wind and said, "The wind is strong because it broke my leg."

"No," said the wind, "the hill is stronger because it can withstand the wind." Ibotity thought it only right that the hill was strongest because it withstood the wind, which split the tree, which broke the leg of Ibotity.

"No," said the hill, "the mouse is stronger because it can burrow into the hill." The mouse denied it. "I can be caught by the cat." Ibotity thought it only right that the cat have the honor of being the strongest because it can catch the mouse, which burrows into the hill, which withstood the wind, which split the tree, which broke the leg of Ibotity.

"No," said the cat, "rope is stronger because it can catch me and tie me up." But rope said no, that it could be cut by iron. "Iron is stronger."

Iron denied it because fire could soften iron. "Ah, I see," said Ibotity, "fire is stronger because it softens the iron, which cuts the rope, which ties the cat, which catches the mouse, which burrows into the hill, which withstood the wind, which split the tree, which broke the leg of Ibotity."

"Not so," said fire, "water quenches." But water said that the canoe was stronger because it cleft the water, and the canoe said that it was split by the rock, and rock said it could be crushed by man.

"Aha," said Ibotity, "man is stronger because he crushes the rock which splits the canoe, which cleaves the water, which quenches the fire, which softens the iron, which cuts the rope, which ties the cat, which catches the mouse, which burrows into the hill, which withstood the wind, which split the tree, which broke the leg of Ibotity."

Shortly there came a distant thunder and the patter of raindrops and Ibotity knew that God had heard his prayer. Moreover, Ibotity knew that God was strongest because he could bring rain to the man who crushes the rock, which overcomes the canoe, which cleaves the water, which quenches the fire, which softens the iron, which cuts the rope, which ties the cat, which caught the mouse, which burrows into the hill, which withstood the wind, which split the tree, which broke the leg of Ibotity.

Story Notes

This circle story has many unique characteristics. Technically it is a chain story with cumulative elements. According to Thompson in *The Folktale* this story has been found in Oriental tale collections and appears frequently in medieval literature. "Though nowhere very popular, nevertheless it has traveled to every continent" (p. 232). Withers retells a Siberian version of this story (pp. 101–102) and Shah refers to Norse, Punjabi, Sri Lankan, Scotch and Irish versions of this tale (p. 94).

This version was developed from several variants, principally Shah's Madagascar tale (p. 94) and Thompson's synopsis of the most well-known story of this type in which the final formula is:

> God how strong you are–God who sends Death, Death who kills blacksmith, blacksmith who makes knife, knife that kills steer, steer that drinks water, water that quenches fire, fire that burns stick, stick that kills cat, cat that eats mouse, mouse that perforates the wall, wall that resists wind, wind that dissolves cloud, cloud that covers sun, sun that thaws frost, frost that broke my foot (p. 232).

The circular aspect was my own invention.

Story Formula

In a time of drought Ibotity climbs a tree to pray, falls and breaks his leg.
Has conversation with elements about who is strongest.
    Ibotity / wind strongest / broke my leg
    Wind / hill stronger / withstood wind
    Hill / mouse stronger / burrows into hill
    Mouse / cat stronger / eats mouse
    Cat / rope stronger / catches and ties cat
    Rope / iron stronger / cuts rope

Iron / fire stronger / softens iron
Fire / water stronger / quenches fire
Water / canoe stronger / cleaves water
Canoe / rock stronger / splits canoe
Rock / man stronger / crushes rock
It begins to rain and Ibotity sees it is God who is strongest because he brings the rain to man.

Other Stories

Another Version

"Who Is Strongest" from *I Saw a Rocket Walk a Mile: Nonsense Tales, Chants and Songs from Many Lands* by Carl Withers, p. 100 (Holt, Rinehart and Winston, 1965).

CHAPTER 6

It Goes On and On and On

The Endless Tale

I'll tell you a story
About Jack a Nory.
I'll tell you another,
About Jack and his brother.
—Nursery Rhyme

Endless stories are always humorous, joking kinds of stories. Elementary age children love them, probably because the children themselves are gaining mastery in language and the joke of the story often relies on the placement of words.

Endless stories are usually simple in form, very short, and of two types. The first type comes quickly to the point and then a single statement is endlessly repeated until the listener calls a halt, as in "Thousands of Ducks." The second type is a round in which the narrative is set up to endlessly repeat, as in "Pete and Repeat" and "A Dark and Stormy Night." The round is much more common in folk songs, but still finds willing tellers in oral form because these stories are more like games or jokes played on the listener—like the catch stories. Sometimes these simple stories are worked into longer stories like "The King Who Loved Stories."

Because endless stories are quite spare, I have not included the story formula unless it seemed appropriate. In most cases, as in "Pete and Repeat," it would be best to memorize the whole. When doing so, it is always a good idea to add your personal touch to stories wherever you can by using animals or people with which you are comfortable. An example where I have done this is "Thousands of Ducks," because my audiences would be most familiar with that type of animal.

THOUSANDS OF DUCKS

Once there was a farmer who owned thousands and thousands of ducks. One day he heard that there was to be a special holiday when lots of people would be in town and willing to buy. Since he had fallen on hard times the farmer decided to take his thousands and thousands of ducks to town to sell.

As he set out for town he came to a wide, wide river. The bridge was far downstream—too far for the ducks to walk. The farmer saw a boat big enough to hold himself and two ducks. So he placed two of the ducks in the boat, climbed in and set off for the other side. When he got the ducks safely to the other side, he rowed back to get two more ducks. He rowed them to the other side and went back for two more ducks. He rowed them to the other side and went back for two more ducks. . . .

(The storyteller pauses. If a listener asks; "What happened?" the teller replies, "He's still getting the ducks.")

Alternate ending: The teller keeps repeating the last line until the listener begs him to stop.

Story Notes

This endless story has a catch. It also has "thousands and thousands" of variants. Depending on the cultural group, the animals might be pigeons or sheep or cattle or ants. The idea is the same in each case— many creatures are going from one point to the next. The teller memorizes the formula line that comes at the end of the story. When telling, begin as if you are telling a marvelous, complex story.

Story Formula

Farmer takes his thousands and thousands of ducks to market,
   comes to stream and must row two over at a time.

After several repetitions, teller pauses and listener asks, "What happened?"

"He's still getting the ducks."

Other Stories

"The Locusts and the Oats" from *I Saw a Rocket Walk a Mile: Nonsense Tales, Chants and Songs from Many Lands* by Carl Withers, p. 48 (Holt, Rinehart and Winston, 1965). A farmer fills his granary with oats, one hole is left at top, room enough for one locust to carry away a grain of oat, then another, etc.

"The Fox and the Geese" in *The Complete Grimm's Fairy Tales*, p. 393 (Pantheon, 1944). In this story a fox wants to eat a flock of geese. They ask him to wait until they have prayed. Then one after the other prays. Tag line: "When they have done praying the story will be continued further, but at present they are still praying unceasingly."

THE KING SLEEPS ON

Once there was a king. Every night the king's storyteller came to him and told him five stories to help him sleep. When the storyteller was done the king slept well. One night after hearing his five stories the king still could not sleep.

"Tell me two more," said the king.

"As the king commands," said the storyteller but he was worried lest the king ask for more stories than he was prepared to tell. He told him two short ones.

The king was all the more restless and asked for a long story . . . a really long story that would help him sleep.

The storyteller wisely began, "Once there was a rich merchant who went to market to buy sheep. He bought one thousand sheep. As he was returning from the fair herding his thousand sheep before him, he came to a river that was so wide the sheep could not pass over. Traveling upstream for a time he came to a part of the river just narrow enough to send three across at a time. And so the man did.

Then he went back and herded three more sheep and then three more sheep," at which point the storyteller fell asleep.

After waiting a few minutes the king woke up the storyteller saying, "Finish the story, please."

"In good time, in good time, your majesty. This river is a large river and the sheep are small, therefore let the merchant bring over all the sheep, then I'll end the story." Seeing the storyteller's cleverly made point that enough was enough the king went to sleep and slept well.

Story Notes

This story is adapted from *A Hundred Merry Tales and Other English Jest Books from the Fifteenth and Sixteenth Century,* P. M. Zall, ed. (Univ. of Nebraska Pr., 1963). Compare this story with "Thousands of Ducks." This variant lets the storyteller sleep while the sheep (locusts, ducks, etc.) cross over. It is a clever adaptation of the story.

Story Formula

King asks for very long story to help him sleep.

King's storyteller tells of farmer bringing a thousand sheep across river, three at a time, then falls asleep.

King wakes him to finish and storyteller says he's waiting for sheep to cross.

Other Stories

See *Other Stories* under "Thousands of Ducks" and "The King Who Loved Stories."

A DARK AND STORMY NIGHT

It was a dark and stormy night as the Captain stood on the bridge and he said to the Mate, "Tell us a yarn."

And the Mate began, "It was a dark and stormy night and the Captain stood on the bridge and said to the Mate, 'Tell us a yarn.'"

And the Mate began, "It was a dark and stormy night and the Captain stood on the bridge and said, 'Tell us a yarn.'"

And the Mate began . . .

Story Notes

Briggs tells us that this well-known tale has variants in every country. Lithuania has 117 variants alone! "The Bear Went Over the Mountain" is a song variant of this concept. You can substitute robbers around their campfire, or soldiers on bivouac, etc.

PETE AND REPEAT

Pete and Repeat were sitting on a fence.
Pete fell off. Who's left?

(*Listeners are supposed to answer at this point*)
Repeat.

Pete and Repeat were sitting on a fence.
Pete fell off. Who's left?

(*The listeners may "get" the joke at this point or not. Carry on until your listeners signal you to stop.*)

Story Notes

This seems a particularly American endless tale. Both Withers (p. 149) and Barton (p. 17) cite versions of the round as a children's game chant. It is a favorite of children since they can join the round and be "in" on the humor.

A MILLION STORIES

I'm going to tell you a million stories. Here is the first one: there were three men in a boat—Harry, Larry and Shut-up. Harry and Larry jumped off. who's left?

(*Listeners respond*) "Shut-up."

Now I am going to tell you a million stories because you told me to shut-up. Here's the first one: There were three men in a boat. . . (*Continue as above or until listeners signal you to stop.*)

Story Notes

A children's chanting story, like "Pete and Repeat," it can be quickly learned. For young children saying "shut up" in the safety of the story, when most have been taught that it is impolite, is part of the fun.

THE TINY GOLD BELL

A rich young man owned a tiny gold bell. He loved its sound and lifted it often to hear the happy tinkle of the tiny gold. One day a shoemaker happened to hear it ring as he entered the young man's house to return some shoes. He asked if he could borrow it for a few days. The young man agreed.

A week passed and the shoemaker had not returned the tiny gold bell, so the young man sent a servant to get the bell. On entering the shoemaker's shop the servant saw the shoemaker's wife and the shoemaker himself dancing to the happy tinkle of the tiny gold bell. The servant could not resist the sight. So happy did the shoemaker seem that the servant joined them in doing a little jig about the shop.

The young man wondered why the servant was taking so long, so he sent another servant. That servant entered the shop and saw the amazing sight of the servant, the shoemaker and his wife dancing and could not keep his toes from tapping to the happy tinkle of the tiny gold bell.

The young man wondered why the servant was taking so long, so he sent another servant. That servant entered the shop and saw the amazing sight of the two servants, the shoemaker and his wife dancing and could not keep his toes from tapping to the happy tinkle of the tiny gold bell.

The young man wondered why the servant was taking so long, so he sent another servant. That servant entered the shop and saw the amazing sight of the three servants, the shoemaker and his wife dancing and could not keep his toes from tapping to the happy tinkle of the tiny gold bell.

Continue until listener calls a stop. Then say . . .

OK. I guess we'll never know how the story ends. Besides, if *we* sent someone to see how it ends, they might stay and dance, too.

Story Notes

This endless tale was inspired by the story description of Motif Z11.6 given in Margaret Read MacDonald's *A Storyteller's Sourcebook: A Subject, Title, and Motif-Index to Folklore Collections for Children* (Neal-Schumann/Gale Research, 1982). The original includes a monk and an apothecary. The whole story can be recast using your own characters. When learning this story be sure to practice the rhythm of the "endless" phrases so there is the feeling for the listener that there will be another development of the plot.

Story Formula

Rich young man has tiny, gold bell, loves sound.

Shoemaker borrows and does not return.

Servant sent to get bell finds shoemaker dancing and cannot resist joining in.

Another servant sent, etc.

"I guess we'll never know how the story ends. Besides, if *we* sent someone to see how it ends, they might stay and dance, too."

Other Stories

Another Version

Fairy Tales from Japan by Miroslav Novak, pp. 193–196 (Hamlyn, 1970).

THE KING WHO LOVED STORIES

Once upon a time there was a king who loved stories. The only thing he loved more was his very beautiful daughter. Many fine men in the kingdom wished to marry her, but the king would only let her marry the one who could tell him so many stories that he would say, "Enough, no more!" Anyone who failed would be beheaded. Many young man lured by her beauty and the chance to be the king's son came to tell their stories so that the king would cry, "Stop!" Alas, all grew tired and hoarse telling their tales night after night until they fell exhausted at the king's feet. They were all beheaded.

One day a poor but honest young man, who had heard of the contest, decided to try. He came to the king and began his tale this way, "There was once a man who built a barn so large that it covered many acres and reached almost to the sky. He filled the barn full of corn to the very top. Unfortunately, he left just one little hole in the top through which there was room for a locust to creep in—just one locust. When he had finished filling the barn there came a locust and fetched one grain of corn. Then another locust came and fetched another grain of corn." The young man went on, saying, "Then another locust came and fetched another grain of corn."

"Yes, yes, so the locust got the grain of corn. Go on."

"Please, your majesty, let me tell the story as it goes. . . . And then another locust came and took another grain of corn. Then another locust came and took another grain of corn."

"Yes, yes, we know the locusts came. Get on with the story."

"Your majesty, my story's only just begun. We must get all the corn from the barn before we can go on."

"Arrgghhh. I grow weary. This tale is endless. Stop! Enough!"

And so it was that young man won the hand of the princess and became a prince himself.

Story Notes

This story was developed from "The Endless Tale: 1" from *A Dictionary of British Folk-tales in the English Language* (Briggs, p. 519) and "The Storyteller" from *Fire on the Mountain and Other Ethiopian Tales* (Courlander, p. 99).

It is a well known formula and varies endlessly from country to country. In Russia there is a version in which a lazy housewife hears too many stories and never gets her work done. Her husband bargains with her not to interrupt a storyteller or she can never listen to another story. In this tale it is an owl who endlessly flies into a well until the housewife cries, "Enough, I have heard about your owl and your well, for the love of Heaven what happened next?", thus losing the bargain. (*Parabola*, Vol. IV, No. 4, p. 38)

Story Formula

King who loved stories has contest for hand of daughter.
Winner must tell stories that make king cry, "Stop! Enough!"
All fail and are beheaded.
Poor young man tells tale of locust taking one grain of corn from
    farmer's barn, then another locust came and took another grain
    of corn, etc. until the king calls a halt.

Other Stories

"The Storyteller," *Fire on the Mountain and Other Ethiopian Tales* by
    Harold Courlander, p. 99 (Holt, Rinehart and Winston, 1950).
"How a Husband Weaned His Wife from Fairy Stories" from *Russian
    Fairy Tales* collected by Aleksandr Afanas'ev, p. 308 (Pantheon
    Books, 1945).

CHAPTER 7

When Is a Story a Story?

The Catch Story

Three wise men of Gotham
Went to sea in a bowl;
If the bowl had been stronger,
My story would have been longer.
—Nursery Rhyme

Catch tales are more like mock stories rather than real ones, and often the teller will use them to tease the audience or to liven up a storytelling session. The form of the catch tale is the same in most instances—the end startles the listener, either by its unexpectedness or abruptness. There are nonsense catch tales such as "The Tail," wherein the ending is unfinished and therefore unexpected; and there are jump stories, such as the well known "In a Dark, Dark House," which startle the listener.

The catch stories are good to have in the repertoire of a beginning storyteller. Occasionally, for one reason or another, an audience may not be paying attention. Telling a catch story, especially if its a scary one, usually brings their attention back to you. The listeners who know the story can join in the game aspect, those who do not are caught awake.

Probably every small child has heard a jump story. I know I did. At camp one summer, when I was about six or seven I heard one about a toe that got buried and the man who wanted it back. I was not expecting the teller to grab me and yell, "Take it," but then, who does. When I giggled, as most do, both from relief and embarrassment, the story had done its work. "My Big Toe" is retold here because it is still a favorite of children.

When telling a jump story, set the listener up for the surprise ending by using a deep, mysterious voice which creates anticipation. Then, at the end, the teller either startles the listener with a quick movement or shouts the punch line or both.

THE TAIL

There was once a shepherd who had many sheep. One day the weather was bad, full of mist and fog, and he had trouble finding his sheep. Finally he found all but one. After searching hill and dale, he found that one too. She had wandered into a swampy area and was up to her tail in water. The shepherd took off his raincoat and bent down, took hold of the sheep's tail and he pulled. But the sheep did not budge, so sodden with water was her fleece. Then the shepherd took off his coat and went in up to his boots in the water. He grabbed hold of the tail and *pulled*. But the sheep was too heavy for him. At last he went in up to his knees and spit on his hands, took a good hold, and he PULLED! and the tail broke. Had that tail been stronger, this tale would be longer.

Story Notes

This unfinished story is Tale Type 2250. Versions of it can be found in Withers (p. 71) and Wiggen's *Tales of Wonder: A Fourth Fairy Book*, p. 321 (Doubleday, 1936). A Scandinavian variant combines both "The Tail" and the box motif in the "Golden Box" with the formula: boy finds box, has key, opens it, finds cow's tail inside. "If that tail had been longer, my tale had been longer."

Story Formula

Shepherd loses all his sheep then finds all but one, which is stuck in a bog.
He takes off his coat, spits on his hands, etc.
Tails breaks, or tale would have been longer.

Other Stories

Another Version:

Just One More by Jeanne Hardendorff, p. 29 (Lippincott, 1969).

HOW YOU TALK!

A farmer went out to his garden one morning to dig up a bunch of potatoes. Taking his digging stick, he began to root up the potatoes when one of the potatoes said, "Oh fine, you don't weed me all summer and now you come around with your digging stick. Leave me alone!"

The farmer turned around and looked at his cow in amazement. The cow was quietly chewing her cud and watching the farmer.

"Did you say something?"

The cow said nothing but the dog spoke up and said, "It wasn't the cow at all but one of your potatoes. The potato said, 'Leave me alone.'"

Now the man had never heard his dog speak before and besides he didn't like the beast's tone. So, he cut a birch switch and got ready to hit him with it when the switch said, "Put me down!"

The man was upset about the way things were going when he lay the switch down on rock and the rock said, "Get that thing off me."

That was enough to totally frighten the man and off he ran down the road, white with fear. He ran into a friend who was coming back from fishing. When the friend saw the farmer looking pretty scared he asked him what was the matter.

Gasping for breath, the words tumbled out of the farmer's mouth, "My potato said, 'Leave me alone', then my dog said 'Listen to the potato', and when I went to whip the dog with a switch, the switch said, 'Put me down' and when I set it on a rock, the rock said, 'Get that thing off me'!"

The friend eyed him suspiciously, "Go on. You're joking!"

"No, every word I said is true. It's the strangest thing I ever saw."

"Now look here," the friend was getting impatient, "dogs and trees and stones don't talk, and I know for certain potatoes don't talk. Now get out of my sight before I lose my temper."

The farmer shrugged and went off. The friend stood looking after him and said aloud to himself, "That is the most ridiculous thing I have ever heard. Imagine thinking things can talk. Nonsense like that gives our town a bad name."

"Ridiculous, isn't it?" said the fish over his shoulder. "Imagine a potato talking."

Story Notes

This kind of story with a surprise ending that is more like "gotcha" than "boo" is known as a "shaggy dog story." Folklorists seem to agree that as a type it got started in the United States and then spread elsewhere. Jan Brunvand, a folklorist who has studied this type of story extensively, defines it as, "A nonsensical joke that employs in the punchline a psychological non sequitur . . . or a hoax to trick the listener who expects conventional wit or wisdom" (p. 114).

Older children, particularly teens, enjoy this type of story.

Story Formula

Farmer, frightened by talking potato, dog, switch, and stone, runs away
Meets friend who has fish over shoulder
Tells friend what has happened
Friend doesn't believe him and sends off farmer
Fish speaks up

Other Stories

Another Version:

"Talk" from *The Cow-Tail Switch and Other West African Stories* by Harold Courlander and George Herzog, p. 25 (Henry Holt and Co., 1947). A longer story with a cumulative chain.

Three Variants:

"The Talking Mule" from *A Treasury of American Folklore*, B. A. Bot-
   kin, ed., p. 440 (Bonanza Books, 1983). An African-American vari-
   ant with mule doing most of the talking.
"The Farmer and His Ox" from *Folktales of England*, Katherine M.
   Briggs and Ruth L. Tongue, ed., p. 140 (University of Chicago
   Press, 1965). A very short version in dialect.
"Tecle's Goat" from *The Fire on the Mountain and Other Ethiopian
   Tales*, by Harold Courlander and Wolf Leslan, p. 93 (Holt, Rine-
   hart and Winston, 1956). The goat talking begins a chain of
   events that ends in saving Tecle's goods.

THE GOLDEN KEY

There once was a boy sent by his mother one morning into the woods
to gather wood for their fire. It was winter time and a deep snow lay
all around. The boy pulled his sleigh through the drifted snow and
managed to gather a good load by afternoon. As he was ready to
return he realized his hands were blue with cold. Fearing frostbite, he
decided to build a fire to warm himself. As he cleared the ground of
snow he came upon an small golden key.

   "If there is a key," he said, "perhaps the lock lies under the snow as
well." Digging further he found an iron box wrought with lovely designs
all over it. He examined it carefully, looking for the lock. At last he found
a small lock and the key exactly fit it. He turned the key around in the
lock, then he turned it around once again. We will have to wait until he
lifts the lid of the box to find what wonderful things might be inside.

Story Notes

This catch story is inspired by Grimm's No. 200, "The Golden Key." It
is a favorite of mine because as the story evolves the listener is drawn
more and more into the details, which create an expectation of something wonderful to come. Thus, in the end the listener is caught by his
own expectation. When telling it you may want to add more of your
own details to create even more suspense.

Story Formula

Boy finds a key, then the box, key fits but we must wait until he
opens it to find what's inside.

Other Stories

Other Versions:

More Tales From Grimm, translated and illustrated by Wanda Gág,
p. ix–x (Coward, McCann, 1947).
The Complete Grimm's Fairy Tales, p. 812 (Pantheon Books, 1944).
Tales of Wonder: A Fourth Fairy Book by Kate Douglas Wiggen, (Doubleday, 1936).

IN A DARK, DARK HOUSE

In a dark, dark house
Is a dark, dark stair
At the top of that dark, dark stair
Is a dark, dark room
In that dark, dark room
Is a dark, dark closet
In that dark, dark closet
Is a dark, dark box
In that dark, dark box
IS A GHOST!

Story Notes

This mock ghost story is a well-known chain chant from England. I
include it here because it is a classic formula tale of its type and is a
perennial favorite of small children. It is the sort of story that should
be in every storyteller's repertoire. It is so very easy to learn because

the premise is so simple and the repetition mostly consisting of "dark, dark."

Other Stories

Other Versions:

"In a Dark Wood" from *The Lore and Language of School Children* by Iona and Peter Opie, p. 36 (Oxford University Press, 1959).

"In a Dark Wood" from *I Saw a Rocket Walk a Mile: Nonsense Tales, Chants and Songs from Many Lands* by Carl Withers, p. 67 (Holt, Rinehart and Winston, 1965).

Other Jump Stories in:

Scary Stories to Tell in the Dark by Alvin Schwartz (J. B. Lippincott, 1981).

Favorite Scary Stories of American Children by Richard and Judy Dockrey Young (August House, 1990).

The Thing at the Foot of the Bed and Other Scary Tales by Maria Leach (World, 1959).

THE TEENY TINY BONE

Once there was a teeny tiny woman who lived in a teeny tiny house at the end of a teeny tiny street. One day she went on a teeny tiny walk with her teeny tiny dog, wearing her teeny tiny coat and her teeny tiny boots.

She happened to walk by a teeny tiny graveyard with her teeny tiny dog and the teeny tiny dog went a teeny tiny way into the grave-yard and began to dig a teeny tiny hole. The teeny tiny woman went to see what the teeny tiny dog had dug up from his teeny tiny hole. She looked down a teeny tiny bit and saw a teeny tiny bone. She picked up the teeny tiny bone and put it in the teeny tiny pocket of her teeny tiny coat and went to her teeny tiny house at the end of the teeny tiny street.

After a teeny tiny while the teeny tiny woman remembered the teeny tiny bone in her teeny tiny coat pocket and said to herself, "I do believe I shall make a teeny tiny pot of soup with my teeny tiny bone." But she realized she was a teeny tiny bit tired and so she put the teeny tiny bone in her teeny tiny cupboard and decided to go upstairs to have a teeny tiny sleep in her teeny tiny bed.

She climbed the teeny tiny stairs in her teeny tiny house and put on a teeny tiny nightgown and climbed into her teeny tiny bed and pulled the teeny tiny covers up to her teeny tiny nose. "Ahhh," she said, "I will just have myself a teeny tiny sleep and be fresh in the morning." At that she closed her teeny tiny eyes and began to sleep, when she heard a teeny tiny voice coming from the teeny tiny cupboard.

"Give me my bone!"

The teeny tiny woman was a teeny tiny bit frightened. She put her teeny tiny head under the teeny tiny covers and went to sleep again. Soon she heard the teeny tiny voice crying.

"Give Me My Bone!"

This made the teeny tiny woman a teeny tiny bit more frightened and she pulled the teeny tiny covers up higher over her teeny tiny head and went to sleep again. When the teeny tiny woman had been asleep a teeny tiny bit more she heard the voice again, a teeny tiny bit louder.

"GIVE ME MY BONE!"

This made the teeny tiny woman a teeny tiny bit more frightened so she pulled her teeny tiny head out from under her teeny tiny covers and in her loudest teeny tiny voice she yelled.

"TAKE IT!"

Story Notes

This jump story has English versions recorded as early as 1843 in *Popular Rhymes and Nursery Tales* by James Orchard Halliwell. There are many variants that use the talking or singing bone motif but this story with its "teeny tiny" repetitions, seems quite similar no matter where it's found. When telling, say "teeny tiny" with a tone that suggests small size to add emphasis and lull them with the repetition so that the end has the desired startling effect.

Story Formula

Teeny tiny woman takes teeny tiny bone and hides it in teeny tiny
   cupboard, etc.
When woman is asleep, voice calls for return of bone three times,
   each time louder: "Give Me My Bone!"
Woman finally yells, "Take It!"

Other Stories

Other Versions:

"Teeny-tiny" in *More English Folk and Fairy Tales* by Joseph Jacobs,
   p. 57 (Putnam, n.d.).

Other Jump Stories:

"Chunk o' Meat" from *Grandfather Tales* by Richard Chase, p. 222
   (Houghton, Mifflin, 1948). This wonderfully ghoulish story is an
   American tale in which an old woman, an old man, and a boy
   find a chunk of meat, take it home, and cook it. A "boogie" comes
   down the chimney to punish them for stealing it. A good jump
   story.
The Tailypo: A Ghost Story is a picture book by Joanna Galdone (Seabury, 1977). A dark story about a creature whose tail gets cut off
   and eaten. The creature returns repeatedly for tail, saying, "You
   know and I know that I gonna get my tailypo." Better for older
   children.
"The Big Toe" from *Scary Stories to Tell in the Dark* by Alvin Schwartz,
   p. 7 (J. B. Lippincott, 1981). A variant of "The Teeny Tiny Woman"
   in which a boy finds a toe sticking out of the ground, cuts off a
   piece of toe and takes it home. Voice follows the boy, asking,
   "Who's got my big toe?" first at door, then on steps, etc. until boy
   yells, "I've got it!" Another longer and more detailed version
   called "The Tale of the Hairy Toe" is told as a legend from North
   Carolina in *Folk Stories of the South* by M. A. Jagendorf, p. 180
   (Vanguard Press, 1972).

CHAPTER 8

Good Things Come in Threes

The Compound
Triad Story

"Third time's the charm"
—Proverb

There were three bears, three bowls, three beds, three chairs, three tries, three pigs, three houses, three wolf-attacks, three questions, three tests of skill, three brothers, three kingdoms, three apples. The recurrence of the number three in folktales is a phenomena that literary scholars and folklorists have mused over for some time. Livo, in *Storytelling Folklore Sourcebook*, defines three as the number of "all," of power, of infinity, of countless numbers (p. 279). Also implied in three is the concept of superlatives: good, better, best; big, bigger, biggest.

There are naturally occurring threes or triads in nature that we know well: morning, noon, and night; birth, life, and death; sun, moon, and stars; heaven, earth, and water. On the human scale, as well, we find triads: mother, father, and child; head, stomach (middle), and feet.

In story, we find one of the most fundamental triads: beginning, middle, and end. Without this triad we have no story. Also, within the story we see a triadic pattern of thesis, antithesis, and synthesis as the action unfolds. An example would be "The Three Little Pigs" in which each of the pigs has a house, one of straw, one of wood, and one of bricks (thesis). The wolf wants to break down the houses and eat the pigs (antithesis) but the third pig saves the other two because his house of bricks withstands the attack and he subsequently destroys the adversary (synthesis).

Many of the folk tales have more than just the basic pattern of three in the plot. There is what folklorist Max Lüthi calls "the fairy tale's own innate stylistic urge towards rigidity of form" and "partiality for certain set numbers: three, seven, twelve, one hundred" (p. 53). What Lüthi is referring to is the tendency in folktales to use number formulas to create meaning.

The value of threes for the storyteller is the ease of remembering sequences and details which are grouped in threes. In fact, Barbara Moran in her article exploring the number three in fairy tales says:

> . . . repetition was essential in orally transmitted tales. It helped listeners remember the story for later retellings, reinforced meaning and offered predictibility. Indeed, by the time Goldilocks starts on Baby Bear's porridge, even the youngest child has figured out what is coming (p. 8).

A story constructed as a simple triad usually has three main events with the recurrence of threes throughout, as in "Partgone, Halfgone and Allgone." Or, as is more often the case, there is a compounding of threes. That is, in the first half there are three events, then a turning point, and three mirroring events in the second half. The result is a wonderful symmetry as in "Goldilocks and the Three Bears" or "The Three Little Pigs." In "The Two Sisters" and "Rumpelstiltskin" we see this compounding of threes.

Folktales which contain triadic clustering are much easier to learn. The outline is simple and, because of the repetition and predictability, it is easy to remember. If you know there is a Papa Bear, then you know there must be Mama Bear and Baby Bear.

This chapter on triads is included in this book on formula tales even though these types of stories are not identified as such by folklorists. The closely kept form, the repetition in such stories makes them consistent with Thompson's definition (see p. 5) of formula tales. However, the concept is mine and evolved as I taught others to tell and learned stories myself for telling. I think you will find this short-hand method of learning stories such as these enjoyable and practical.

RUMPELSTILTSKIN

Once upon a time in a kingdom far away there was a king who valued gold above all else. In his kingdom there was a miller who would often brag to get the better of his friends. One day he bragged so outrageously that even the king heard of it.

"I have a daughter who can spin straw into gold!"

The king heard of this marvel and ordered the girl brought to his castle. When she arrived he took her into a room piled from floor to ceiling, ceiling to floor with straw.

"Spin all this straw into gold by morning or I shall lock you away forever," said the king.

He turned and went out, locking the door behind him. The girl sat on the stool before the spinning wheel, and tried with all her might to spin the gold and at last she cried, "Boo-hoo, I don't know what to do."

Without the door ever opening, in came a funny little man with long, bony fingers, long, bony toes and a long, bony nose. He came with a *hunchety-hunchety* kind of walk.

"What will you give me if I spin your straw into gold, miller's daughter?"

"Why I have this ring, will you take it?"

The creature put the ring in his pocket and sat on the stool. Taking straw into his long, bony hands he began to spin, *whir, whir*. In no time at all he had spun all the straw into shimmering, shining threads of gold that hung everywhere about the room.

In the morning the king returned and saw all the gold. "This pleases me well, miller's daughter. Come with me." He took the girl into another room, larger than the first. It too was piled from ceiling to floor, floor to ceiling with straw.

"Spin all this straw into gold by morning or I shall lock you away forever."

He went out and locked the door behind him. The girl sat on the stool and tried again to spin the dry straw into wonderful gold and at last cried, "Boo-hoo, I don't know what to do."

Without the door ever opening, in came that creature, *hunchety-hunchety*.

"What will you give me if I spin this straw into gold, miller's daughter?"

"I have a necklace. Will you take that?"

The creature put the necklace in his pocket and sat on the stool. Taking straw into his long, bony hands he began to spin, *whir, whir*. In no time at all he had spun all the straw into shimmering, shining threads of gold that hung everywhere about the room.

In the morning the king came back and saw all the gold. "This pleases me well. Come with me, miller's daughter." He took her into a third room, bigger than the first two. It was piled from ceiling to floor, floor to ceiling with straw.

"Spin all this straw into gold by morning and I will make you my queen."

He went out and locked the door behind him. The girl sat on the stool and tried even harder to spin the gold herself and at last cried,

"Boo-hoo, I don't know what to do."

Into the room, without the door ever opening came that strange little man, *hunchety-hunchety*.

"What will you give me if I spin this straw into gold?"

"I have nothing left to give you."

"Not so," said the creature with a wily look. "When you are queen you could give me your firstborn child."

Unfortunately, the girl agreed to this bargain. The creature sat on the stool. Taking straw into his long, bony hands he began to spin, *whir, whir*. In no time at all he had spun all the straw into shimmering, shining threads of gold that hung everywhere about the room.

In the morning when the king came back and saw all the gold he said, "This pleases me well."

He married the miller's daughter and made her his queen. One year later, a child was born and the new queen was delighted. Until one day, into the room, without the door ever opening, came that strange little man, *hunchety-hunchety*.

"I've come for the child." He reached out with his long, bony hands. The queen cried, "No! Surely you'll take something else instead?"

With that same wily look he said, "I shall play a game with you—a name game. If in three days time you can guess my name, the child is yours. If you do not, the child is mine. Agreed?"

"Agreed," said the queen.

The queen sent out her guards into all the kingdom, asking all the rich and high born, "Do you know who the creature is? Do you know his name?"

When the creature returned the next day he asked the queen his name.

"Is it Agamemnon?"

"No."

"Is it Mankelman?"

"No."

"Is it Aboodabah?"

"No." The queen sighed because she had no more names.

"Two more days, Queen."

The queen sent out her guards into all the surrounding villages and barnyards, asking, "Do you know who the creature is? Do you know his name?"

When the creature returned the second day he asked the queen his name.

"Is it Sheepshanks?"

"No."

"Is it Cowface?"

"No."

The queen sighed because she had no more names.

"One more day, Queen."

The queen sent out her guards into the whole world. No one could find the name of the creature. Just at sundown the captain of the guard came riding fast to the castle steps. Jumping from his horse and bowing low he said, "Madame, I have traveled the world over to find the name of the creature. I could not, until I passed through a dark wood. In the middle of the wood was a hut with a fire in front. Dancing around the fire was the strangest little man with long, bony fingers, long bony toes, and a long bony nose. He was dancing around the fire and singing—

Today I bake
Tomorrow I brew
The next I'll have the young queen's child
Glad I am that no one knew
That Rumpelstiltskin I am styled

The queen was ready for the creature. The next day he came in *hunchety-hunchety.* "What is my name, queen?"

"Is it Rumpelstiltskin?"

"Someone told you! Someone told you!" The creature stomped his foot in such a rage it broke through the floor and he had to take both hands to pull it out. Everyone thought him so ridiculous they laughed him out of the castle and out of the kingdom all together. As for the queen and her child, they lived happily ever after.

Story Notes

This famous story about a strange little man who's name must be learned to overpower him can be found in many variants. He has been termed by folklorists as the "solitary impet." In Britain he is known as Tom Tit Tot, Perifool, and Terrytop; in Norway he is Skaane, Whuppity Stoorie; in Scotland he is Titty Tod; Gilitrutt in Iceland; and Rompeltailskin in Louisiana.

This story is one of the early stories I learned to tell. Its easy to learn because of its compound structure and the repetition of threes: three times the girl must spin, three times the little man comes to help, three things are demanded in payment. The first half of the story leads up to the transforming event, the girl becoming queen and having a child. Then, the little man comes to collect his wages.

This telling is based on the 1857 version of the Grimm's story (No. 55). When I tell this story I invite involvement by teaching the children the sounds as I go—*whir, whir* and *hunchety, hunchety*—as well as the refrain "He has long bony fingers, long bony toes and a long bony nose." All the rhyming phrases, except the little man's song, are my addition and add music to the story.

For ideas about what gold spun from straw might look like, read the marvelous Caldecott honors picture book, "Rumpelstiltskin" (E. P. Dutton, 1986). Author Paul Zelinsky's illustrations of the tale are set in medieval Europe. Every picture is rich with color and detail. As a teller, you can include word description from the book that would enhance the telling. If you would like to tell "Rumpelstiltskin," but think it is too familiar, you are probably wrong! Usually, audiences know *about* the story but have never heard a telling. This is especially true of school-age children. If you tell this one, feel confident you will find a receptive audience.

Story Formula

1st Triad

1. Miller's bragging and king's greed force miller's daughter to perform three impossible tasks of spinning straw into gold in big, bigger, biggest room.
2. Miller's daughter cries, brings supernatural helper (little man) three times to spin straw.

3. Little man receives three gifts: ring, necklace, promise of firstborn child.

Transforming event

By performing all three impossible tasks, the miller's daughter is taken from her lowly position, made a queen and bears a child.

2nd Triad

1. The little man returns for child, queen protests, he makes a bargain that she must guess his name to keep the child. She is given three chances.

2. Three times the queen sends out her guards to learn the name, sends them to: neighborhood, kingdom, whole world.

3. Three times the little man returns. Queen guesses three names each time except last.

Conclusion

Having lost the bargain Rumpelstiltskin puts his foot through floor and, looking ridiculous, he is laughed out of kingdom.

Other Stories

Variants of Rumpelstiltskin:

"Tom Tit Tot" from *English Fairy Tales* by Joseph Jacobs, p. 9 (Penguin Books, 1971). In this version a girl's mother brags to the king that her daughter can spin five skeins in a day. "A small, little black thing" helps her three times. Ending refrain: "Nimmy nimmy not. My name's Tom Tit Tot."

"Whuppity Stoorie" from *Tattercoats and Other Folktales* (Harvey House, 1986). This version has a feminine supernatural helper. An old woman in green performs a cure in exchange for "whatever she wants," which is the woman's child. Woman has three days to guess the name, overhears in woods.

PARTGONE, HALFGONE, ALLGONE

Bear, Fox and Rabbit were friends, real good friends, and one day they decided to cook up a big pot of pea soup at Rabbit's house. After it was bubbling and simmering on the stove, they all went down to the river to have a nap.

Of course, Rabbit went, too, but all the time he was thinking about that pea soup and how good it would taste. When they had all settled down under a big cedar tree on the riverbank, Rabbit could stand it no longer.

"I think I hear my wife calling me." He went to the house and helped himself to a big bowl of soup. "Mmmm, smackin' good!"

When he got back to the river bank he smiled real big and said his wife had just given birth. Bear and Fox asked him what they had decided to name the baby.

"Partgone," said Rabbit.

A little more time passed on the river bank, Rabbit kept thinking about that soup and how good it tasted.

"I believe I hear my wife calling me again. Maybe she had twins." He went to the house and ate some more soup. Then he headed back to the riverbank. Fox and Bear asked, "Was it twins?"

"Yes, sir, it was twins. This one we are going to call Halfgone."

Bear and Fox thought Partgone and Halfgone were very strange names for Rabbit's children, but they were polite and didn't say anything. Pretty soon Rabbit was thinking about that soup again. "Oh, smackin' good it was," he said to himself.

"I am sure I hear my wife calling me again."

Bear and Fox were starting to get suspicious. "I don't hear anything," growled Bear.

"Oh, it's my wife all right. She must be having triplets. I'll go see her and be right back."

Rabbit high-tailed it for home and licked the pot of soup clean. He came back, smiling big as you please.

"Well, it's true. My wife had triplets and we're calling the third one Allgone."

By then it was time for dinner and Fox and Bear were hungry. They went into Rabbit's house and found the soup gone. Then, they went looking for Rabbit but he was 'allgone,' too.

Story Notes

This story was based on an African-American story by the same name collected and published in the *Journal of American Folklore* (Vol. 4, No.

184, 1934) by Ralph Steele Boggs. This story has many counterparts around the world: African, Scandanavian, Native American (Menominee), European (German) to name a few. The joke varies only slightly in the wording of the names of the children or in what is eaten.

This story is an example of a simple triad in which Rabbit returns three times to eat the soup. The structure is implied even in the title. Note there is no mirroring effect as in "Rumpelstiltskin" or the following story, "Two Sisters." When practicing this story, tell it as if naming the babies Partgone, Halfgone, and Allgone were perfectly normal. You will find your timing in delivering the line will be better using this technique.

Story Formula

Precipitating event
Bear, Rabbit and Fox make a pot of soup, then leave the house.
1st Episode
Rabbit goes to house to eat soup under guise of seeing his wife who he says is having a baby.
Returns, tells other two he named the child Partgone.
2nd Episode
Rabbit goes again to house to eat soup.
Returns, tells other two he named the child Halfgone.
3rd Episode
Rabbit goes third time to house to eat soup.
Returns, tells other two he named the child Allgone.
Ending
Bear and Fox discover soup is gone and Rabbit is 'allgone.'

Other Stories

Another Version:

"Cat and Mouse in Partnership" from *The Complete Grimm's Fairy Tales*, No. 2, p. 21 (Pantheon Books, 1944).

A Variant:

"Presentneed, Bymeby and Hereafter" from *Grandfather Tales* by
Richard Chase, p. 140 (Houghton, Mifflin, 1948). A man and his
wife have a misunderstanding of the three phrases of the title.
This story is not so much similar to "Partgone, Halfgone and
Allgone," as it is similar in the formula of threes and hinges on a
play on words.

THE TWO SISTERS

Once there were two sisters, Blanche and Rose, who lived with their
widowed mother in a small cottage in a small village far from here.
The older sister was as mean-spirited and ugly as the younger one
was kind and sweet-looking. Now the mother favored Blanche, no
doubt because she was as mean and ugly as herself. Blanche wore
pretty dresses and went to parties. Rose was made to clean and haul
water.

One day the mother sent Rose to sit by the well and spin a huge bag
of wool. She was told not to come home until it was done. Rose
worked her spindle till late in the afternoon. Her fingers began to
bleed from the hard work they had done. Rose leaned over into the
well to wash her hands when the spindle dropped in.

When she returned home with her spinning undone and her spindle lost her mother flew into a rage and told her to go back to the well
immediately and get the spindle.

Sobbing, Rose returned to the well and tried to fish out the spindle
but could not. In despair she threw herself in after it. Darkness covered her for a time and when she awoke she was in a beautiful meadow full of sunlight and flowers of every color. There was a mown path
through the meadow which Rose followed until she came to a cow
with a pail and a milking stool.

"Please milk me for my bag is full."

"Certainly," said Rose. And immediately she sat down and milked
the cow, who thanked her as she went. Soon she came to an apple tree
heavy with ripe, red apples, a ladder and a basket.

"Please pick me, for my apples are all ripe," said the tree.

"Of course," said Rose and scurried up the ladder and picked all the ripe apples. The tree thanked her as she went. Soon she came to a baker's brick oven full of bread brown from the baking and a wooden paddle.

"Please pull us from the oven for we are all done."

"With pleasure," said Rose and she swung the paddle up and scooped up all the loaves and set them to cool. The bread thanked her as she went.

Finally Rose came to a lovely cottage all full of green ivy and flowers growing all about. She looked into the window and saw a fierce looking woman with long teeth. Frightened, the girl began to run away when the woman spoke.

"What are you afraid of, child. Stay with me, do your work well and it will not go ill with you. But, you must take care to make my feather bed just right. Each morning you must shake it till the feathers fly—then there will be snow on earth. I am Mother Holle."

The old woman spoke so kindly that Rose could not refuse and so she stayed. Rose did everything to Mother Holle's satisfaction, and always shook her feather bed to make the snow on earth. In return, the woman fed her wonderful meats and cakes.

Even so, Rose grew lonesome for her life above and asked the woman to release her from her service. Mother Holle agreed and said, "Just as you have served me well, I will serve you well." She led Rose to a great carved door in the meadow. When Rose opened it she could see the other world she knew, the well and beyond it her cottage. Mother Holle handed her the spindle she had lost and said good-bye. As Rose stepped through the door a shower of gold fell on her, and when she gave a startled cry, gold fell from her mouth.

Joyfully she ran to her mother's house. As she entered the yard the rooster called out:

"Cock-a-doddle-doo!

Your golden girl's come back to you!"

When her mother and Blanche saw all the gold she carried, Rose was welcomed by them. And, when she told them all that had happened, they were even more amazed at the story and at the gold falling from her lips.

That night Blanche and her mother hatched a plot to get the same rewards for Blanche.

The next morning Blanche set out for the well. She simply threw the spindle down the well.

"I'll not hurt my lovely hands spinning."

Then she jumped in after and awoke in the meadow. Seeing the path she walked as fast as she could. When she came to the cow, it said:

"Please milk me for my bag is full."

"Milk you! I have better things to do."

Further down the path she came to the apple tree:

"Please pick me for my apples are all ripe."

"Pick you! Why should I dirty my hands?"

On she went down the path till she came to the baker's brick oven:

"Please take us from the oven, for we are all brown."

"Take you from the oven! I have no time."

Coming at last to the old woman's cottage she poked her head through the window and said:

"You must be Mother Holle. I have come to work for you." And immediately she let herself in. At first, Blanche was diligent but soon she did not bother to shake the feather bed or sweep the floor. Mother Holle grew tired of her bad attitude and told her to go. Blanche was sure it was time to get her gold.

Mother Holle led her to the door also, but when she stepped through black tar covered her. When she opened her mouth to give a startled cry, frogs came out. When she ran crying into the yard, the cock called out:

"Cock-a-doddle-doo!

Your dirty girl's come back to you!"

Blanche could not get the tar off her as long as she lived and she seldom talked because of the frogs. As for Rose, a prince married her and they are living happily ever after.

Story Notes

Known as Tale Type 480: *The Kind and Unkind Girls*, Thompson calls this story type one of the most popular oral tales in the whole world, with variants being found in almost every culture (p. 126). In the *Type-Index* Aarne and Thompson group the stories under the "spindle and well" type and the "journey" type where emphasis is on the encounters with animals and objects.

This story is the "spindle and well" type and is based on Grimms' "Frau Holle" (No. 24) and Perrault's "The Fairy" (Opie, p. 129). Note the beautiful symmetry that allows the cautionary word of the story to shine forth: what you do to others rebounds back on yourself. I prefer this version of the tale to the second group because of the implied notion that there is another world under this one that influences such things as weather.

There is speculation about who Mother Holle is. Thompson refers to her as a witch, Chase as a mean old woman, and others as an earth spirit. I prefer to think of her as the personification of Mother Earth or Mother Nature.

The story's compound structure helps make clear the lesson—this is what happens when you do well and this is what happens when you do not. Children understand the story's truth intuitively. I often hear them gasp when Blanche does not help the cow, the apple tree, and the loaves. When telling this story maintain the rhythms in the dialogue, even if you create your own. These rhythms are like the harmony to the plot's melody and add to the overall effect.

Story Formula

Precipitating Event

Two sisters, Blanche and Rose: one is ugly and mean, the other fair and sweet. Mother favors Blanche and sends Rose to spin at the well.

1st Triad

1. Rose loses spindle, falls in after it, and discovers other world.
2. Performs three tasks asked: milk cow, pick apples, remove loaves from oven.
3. Meets Mother Holle and works hard for her, until Rose returns through door into upper world. Receives shower of gold and gold when she speaks.

Transforming event

Rose returns and Blanche and mother are jealous of her reward. Mother sends Blanche to get same.

2nd Triad

1. Blanche throws spindle in well and jumps in after.
2. Refuses to perform the three tasks asked: milk cow, pick apples, remove loaves from oven.

3. Meets Mother Holle and doesn't work hard, asked to leave through same door. Receives shower of tar and frogs when she speaks.
   Conclusion
Rose marries a prince, lives happily.

Other Stories

"Gallymanders! Gallymanders!" from _Grandfather Tales_ by Richard Chase, p. 18 (Houghton, Mifflin, 1948). This story was collected in the mountains of Kentucky, but the theme of the kind and unkind girls is the same. Each is running from the old woman and given three tasks by a tree, a cow and an oven. The refrain is repeated three times for each girl:

> "Gallymanders! Gallymanders!
> All my gold and silver's gone,
> My great long money purse!"

The Talking Eggs retold by Robert D. San Souci (Dial Books, 1989). A rich retelling of a Louisiana Cajun version of the kind and unkind girls. Blanche and Rose are each given three tasks and are rewarded accordingly.

"Toads and Diamonds" from _Twenty-Two Splendid Tales to Tell_, by Pleasant DeSpain, p. 21 (August House, 1994) or _The Blue Fairy Book_ by Andrew Lang, p. 295 (Longmans, Green, 1929). Both versions are retellings of Perrault's "The Fairy," but DeSpain's version is charming and very easy to learn.

A WORLD OF FOOLS

Once there was a girl named Polly and a boy named Jack who were to get married. Jack loved Polly more than anything. He loved her for many reasons, but most of all he loved her cleverness.

"Why she can see the wind coming up the street and hear a fly cough," boasted Jack to all his friends.

As their wedding day drew near, Polly and her parents invited Jack to dinner one evening. When they had all seated themselves, Polly's father said, "Polly, will you go down to the cellar and draw some cider from the barrel?"

"Of course," said Polly and promptly picked up a pitcher and went down the cellar stairs. As she placed the pitcher under the barrel and turned the tap, her eyes fell on a pick ax buried in the wood above her head. She began to think about that pick ax a great deal.

"What if, when Jack and I are married, we have a baby and that baby gets old enough to draw cider from the barrel and that pick ax should fall on him and kill him?" The very thought of this made Polly cry and wail. The cider continued to fill the pitcher and pour onto the floor. Polly paid no attention. She was thinking only of the child who would have the pick ax fall on him and die.

When Polly didn't return Polly's mother went down to see what had happened to her. She found Polly up to her ankles in cider.

"Polly, whatever is the matter?"

"Oh, mother, you would cry too if you were me," wailed Polly, "See that pick ax? If Jack and I get married and have a child and that child comes down to draw cider from the barrel, the pick ax will fall on his head and kill him."

Polly's mother immediately saw the awful predicament and began to weep as well. "Oh waaaaaaaa, my grandchild, my poor, poor grandchild." Meanwhile, the cider continued to flow from the barrel.

When Polly's father came down to see where his wife and daughter were, they were above their ankles in cider, crying big crocodile tears.

"What on earth is the matter with you two?"

"You would cry too, husband, if you knew the awful truth. Look." Polly's mother pointed to the pick ax. "If Jack and Polly get married and have a child and that child comes down to draw cider from the barrel, the pick ax will fall on his head and kill him."

When Polly's father saw the truth of it, he began at first to sniffle and then to cry. Jack was sitting alone upstairs waiting for Polly, Mother, and Father but no one came. Finally, he too descended the stairs and saw all three weeping and wailing and up to their knees in cider.

"What on earth is the matter with you three?"

Polly's father pointed to the pick ax and said, "If you and Polly get married and have a child and that child comes down to draw cider from the barrel, the pick ax will fall on his head and kill him. I will lose my first grandchild. Ohh, boo-hoo-hoo."

"You can't be serious," Jack said, astonished at the three people sitting in cider, weeping and wailing for something that may never happen. "I don't think I have ever seen three more foolish people in the whole world. I am not so sure I want to be married to so foolish a girl. In fact, I am going to walk until my shoes wear out and if I can find three people more foolish than you before my feet are bare, I'll marry my sweetheart."

Jack set out immediately walking down the road and it wasn't long before he came to a farmer shoveling and sweating, sweating and shoveling nothing but thin air.

"What are you doing," Jack asked.

"I am shoveling sunbeams into the barn to help the corn ripen."

"Why don't you bring the corn out into the sun?"   .

The farmer brightened with a delighted smile. "Why I never thought of that. What a clever idea. Thank you so much!"

Jack knew that he had found his first fool. It wasn't long before he came to another farm where a woman was trying to lift a cow up over her head and onto the hill.

"Good grief, woman, what are you doing?"

"I want to feed the cow the grass that grows on the hill and the hill is too steep for her to climb."

"Why don't you cut the grass and bring it to her?"

The woman beamed with joy and thanked him. Jack had found his second great fool. He traveled only a short way when he saw a man standing on his front porch in his undershorts with a pair of pants on the chair. Every little while he would run and jump trying to get into the pants. Jack laughed at the silly sight and knew he had found his third fool and it was still morning.

At last he turned back to find his own sweet Polly, his first fool, because he knew that the world was full of fools.

Story Notes

This compound triad is a favorite story of many peoples, probably because they recognize themselves in the portrayal of the universal human tendency to borrow trouble before it comes. There are variants from such diverse places as Jamaica—where it is an Anansi the

Spider story—to Norway, England, Germany. This story is based on two versions, "Three Fools and More" from a retelling in the *Detroit Free Press* (March 30, 1993, p.4D) and "The World of Fools" from the *Journal of American Folklore* (Vol. 47, No. 87/Oct.–Dec. 1934).

Story Formula

Jack is to marry Polly. At dinner Polly goes to cellar to get cider.

1st Triad

1. Polly, 2. Mother, and 3. Father each go to cellar for cider and see pick ax, imagine future child will be killed and begin to sob.

Transforming event

Jack vows not to marry Polly unless he finds three bigger fools than Polly and her parents. He sets out to find them.

2nd Triad

Jack finds:

1. Farmer shoveling sunbeams to ripen corn.
2. Farm wife lifting cow to high meadow for grass.
3. Man trying to put on trousers by jumping into them.

Other Stories

Other Versions:

Jack and the Three Sillies by Richard Chase (Houghton, Mifflin, 1950). This picture book is a chain story paired with a triad. The first half is similar to "Hans In Luck" (p. 28); in this "swapping story" the main character, Jack, keeps trading down, each exchange being for something of less value. In the second half, Jack's wife is disgusted with Jack's bad bargaining and goes in search of three people sillier than he.

"Clever Elsie" from *The Complete Grimm's Fairy Tales*, No. 34 (Pantheon Books, 1944). Elsie marries Hans after the ax-head scenes, and Hans discovers to his dismay that "clever" Elsie is as big a fool after the wedding as before.

"The Three Sillies" from *English Fairy Tales* by Joseph Jacobs, p. 10 (Penguin, 1971).

"Clever Gretchen" from *Clever Gretchen and Other Forgotten Tales* by-Alison Laurie, p. 1 (Thomas Y. Crowell, 1980). This story is a more recent retelling of the Joseph Jacobs version, "The Three Sillies."

THE THREE RABBITS

Once upon a time there were three rabbits who lived in a deep and narrow hole with their mother and father. One day father said to the three, "Little rabbits, pick up yours ears and listen to me. You are now one month old and the time has come for you each to go and dig your own run to live in. This night your brothers and sisters will be born and the hole is too small for all of us. It is the way of rabbits. Your mother and I did the same. When you choose a hole make it long and narrow and close to us so we can see each other."

When the three rabbits were ready to leave they said good-bye and went out into the world, each going their own way. The first rabbit said, "Oh, yuck, I hated that dark, damp run we lived in. I'm going to build a lovely cottage in the sunlight and come and go as I please."

The first rabbit did just that. He collected some fresh leaves and moss and made the nicest house. When it was done, he hopped out into the nearby meadow and began to nibble some tender grass. Just then a fox trotted up to him and said, "Oh little rabbit, how good it is to see you. Let's sit down together and talk."

"Ha," said the first rabbit. "I am no fool. You want to eat me up, but you won't." He hippity-hopped away into his little house of moss and twigs, feeling quite safe. In a matter of minutes the fox bounded over, pulled down the house and ate the rabbit.

The second rabbit also said to himself, "That run we lived in was much too long and narrow. I don't want to do all that digging for no reason. I will build my house in the roots of trees and be quite safe and have the sunshine on my whiskers as often as I please."

The second rabbit gathered twigs and ferns and made a soft burrow just under the roots of a tree. When it was done, he hopped out into the meadow and began to nibble on some tender grass. The fox had been watching him and trotted up.

"Good afternoon, friend rabbit. I see you are new to the neighborhood. Can we be friends?"

"I am no friend of yours, fox. You only want to eat me up, but you won't." The second rabbit hippity-hopped into his burrow under the roots of the tree and felt quite safe. In no time the fox bounded after him, threw aside the twigs and dug down under the roots and ate the rabbit.

The third rabbit said to himself: "I am going to build near my father's house but I will do him one better. I will dig a tunnel longer and narrower than his." He dug a long winding run and when it was done he went inside and hid himself until he needed food. Out in the meadow, sure enough, he met the fox.

"Hello, my little friend. Come closer and let's talk."

"You cunning old fox. Don't you think I heard from the other animals that yesterday you ate my brothers? You may gobble them, but you won't gobble me."

The third rabbit hippity-hopped into his narrow, twisty lair and waited. The fox bounded up to the hole and tried every which way to get in. Finally, he had to give up. And that was the end of that.

Story Notes

You will of course recognize this variant of the favorite story "The Three Little Pigs." A simple triad in structure, it is a Turkish tale adapted from "The Three Hares" (Cole, p. 497). Your audience will love this story, since they will be "in the know" early on in the telling; yet, the surprise variants, such as the first two rabbits getting eaten, will keep them involved.

Story Formula

Three young rabbits go out to build their runs, first two ignore
    father's warning to dig a long and narrow run:

1st Rabbit: builds a house above ground, with twigs and moss—eaten by fox.

2nd Rabbit: builds house just under tree roots with sticks and ferns—eaten by fox.

3rd Rabbit: builds house narrower and longer than father's—escapes fox.

Other Stories

Variants:

"The Story of the Three Little Pigs" from *English Fairy Tales* by Joseph Jacobs, p. 69 (Penguin, 1971). There are a great many copies of this story in collections and picture books.

"The Three Little Piggies" from *Why the Possum's Tail is Bare and Other Classic Southern Stories,* collected by Jimmy Neil Smith, p. 177 (Avon Books, 1993). A humorous Southern telling of the old favorite which begins with an "old sow and her three sons—Tom, Will and Jack."

Other Compound Triad Stories

"Scrapefoot" from *More English Folk and Fairy Tales* by Joseph Jacobs, p. 94 (Putnam, n.d.). A variant of "The Three Bears" in which Scrapefoot, a wolf, sneaks into the Three Bears' castle and enjoys the food and furniture.

"The Story of the Three Bears" from *English Fairy Tales* by Joseph Jacobs, p. 96 (Penguin, 1971). The original Robert Southey version in which a dishonest old woman comes to steal the porridge and try the furniture.

"The Cat, the Cock and the Fox" from *Russian Fairy Tales,* by Aleksander Afanas'ev, trans. by Norbert Guterman, p. 86 (Pantheon Books, 1945).

"Salt" from *Russian Fairy Tales,* by Aleksandr Afanas'ev, trans. by Norbert Guterman, p. 40 (Pantheon Books, 1945). Or a picture book version: *Salt* by Harve Zemach (Follett Publishing, 1965).

CHAPTER 9

I Wonder

The Question Story

Hard questions must have hard answers.
—Plutarch

The question story poses a dilemma, then asks how it might be resolved. Depending on the intent of the story and the culture it derives from, the story may have only one answer, such as in "King Solomon's Test" or it may have a variety of possible answers arrived at from discussion with the listeners as in "The Leftover Eye."

The latter type of question story with more than one possible answer is usually both simple and complex. This type of story's simplicity lies in its brief description of the problem in narrative form. Its complexity lies in the range of thought required to arrive at a solution. Answers are not simply yes or no. In fact, the answers are more likely *yes and no.*

Which ever emphasis you choose you will find that children and adults enjoy the question story, if presented in the right way. Making a game of the story is the best approach.

Peoples such as West African Ashanti and Hasidic Jews use the question story extensively and see it as an essential tool for analytical and creative thinking. The Ashanti revere wisdom and cultivate a thoughtful approach to life even in the very young. However, a story such as "The Leftover Eye" is often reserved for adolescence and upwards. In fact, stories like "The Leftover Eye" are debated and discussed for years, even generations. The elders arrive at a better understanding of human nature by continuing to explore other possible outcomes of the stories.

KING SOLOMON'S TEST

In ancient times, when wise King Solomon ruled, it was said that there was no question he could not answer, no riddle he could not solve.

In the lands far to the south of Israel lived the queen of Sheba. She was known for her skill and intelligence. She had often heard of King Solomon's fabled wisdom and she began to wonder, "Is he really as wise as people say?" She decided to test him and see for herself.

She sent a messenger telling King Solomon that the Queen was coming to visit. In a large caravan of elephants and horses, she traveled by land and sea to reach Jerusalem.

Upon entering the shining palace she ordered her servants to lay before the King her gifts. They were a wonder to behold. There were the greater gifts—a lamp that when rubbed would grant you anything you wished, a ring that when worn would let you understand the speech of animals and a carpet that would fly you to the far corners of the earth. Then came the lesser gifts—a chest of diamonds, a chest of rubies and a chest of emeralds. All these things she laid before the King. He looked in wonder at them and said, "So many great gifts. What can I give you in return, Queen from the South?"

"I only come to do you honor. But, it would please me if you granted me one tiny request."

"Anything, name it."

"Aid me in settling an argument." At that she clapped her hands and two servants came forward, each bearing a pillow with a lily laying on it.

The Queen pointed to the two flowers and said, "Great King Solomon, You see before you two lilies. One was plucked from the field this very morning, the other was made by the hand of a master craftsman. Which is the true lily?"

Solomon looked from one flower to the other. To his eye they looked identical, so cleverly was one made.

(At this point pause and say to the audience, "If this problem came to you what would you do?" Allow the audience to respond with possible ways to test for the real flower: smell it, touch it, etc. Then pick up the story again.)

There was a great silence in the throne as Solomon studied the problem. Those in attendance on the King began to wonder if he was finally stumped. Then King Solomon stood up and drew back a curtain from an open window. Soon there came a sound of bzzzzzzzzzzzz. A servant rushed forward to kill a bee that had flown in through the open window. Solomon said, "Let the bee alone."

Everyone watched at the bee hovered over the two lilies and landed on the second flower.

"This is the true lily," said Solomon.

"It is indeed," said the Queen of Sheba, bowing before him. "And you are as wise as people say. It is a wise man indeed who is willing to learn from even the humble honeybee."

Story Notes

This story is reprinted from my book *Storytelling: A Creative Teaching Strategy* (Storytime Productions, 1985) and is based on a Jewish legend that is one of a whole series of King Solomon stories in the Jewish oral tradition. King Solomon is thought to be the consummate wise man of both story and real life. He was an actual Jewish king who ruled from 965–925 B.C. and whose legendary wealth and the extent of his influence has not been equaled even by today's standard of prosperity. Because he asked God to give him wisdom to be able to rule the Jewish nation instead of asking for wealth or power, the Bible tells us he was given wisdom, wealth *and* power. In the Jewish oral tradition, Solomon is portrayed as having many supernatural abilities—to ride a magic carpet wherever there is a need for him, to understand and speak to animals, and to read people's thoughts.

"King Solomon's Test" is a story with one correct answer (though I have had students say there are other ways to solve the problem). Because of this, there may be students who know the correct answer already. To forstall having someone call out the answer, I say at the beginning, "This is a story with a problem. I am going to stop at a certain point and ask you to solve it. If you already know the answer, why don't you keep it a secret and let the others have the fun of figuring it out." That usually is the end of the matter.

When allowing the audience to call out possible ways to figure out which is the true lily, I usually get: "smell it" or "touch it" or "let it fade." With each response I act it out as if it were part of the story. This usually keeps interest very high. When I get either a correct answer or no one can figure it out, I resume: "The story goes on to say . . . "

Story Formula

The Queen of Sheba tests King Solomon's fabled wisdom by
   presenting two lilies—one real and one crafted—and asking him
   to choose the real one.
He allows a bee to discover the real one.

Other Stories

Other Versions:

"Which Flower" from *Stories to Solve* by George Shannon, p. 20
   (Greenwillow, 1985).
"The Wisdom of Solomon" from *Twenty-Two Splendid Tales to Tell* by
   Pleasant DeSpain, p. 17 (August House, 1994).

Other King Solomon Stories

The Carpet of Solomon by Sulamith Ish-Kishor (Pantheon Books,
   1966). A lovely telling of King Solomon's magic carpet adven-
   tures.
"The Old Man, the Snake and the Judgement of Solomon" from *A
   Treasury of Jewish Folklore*, edited by Nathan Ausubel, p. 70
   (Crown Publishers, 1948). King Solomon as a young boy delivers
   wise judgement on behalf of the old man and betters his father,
   King David.

THE LEFTOVER EYE

This is a story of things that never happened. But if it were possible
for such things to happen, it would have happened.
   This is the tale of a man who was blind. His mother, too, was blind.
And, can you believe it, his wife and his wife's mother were blind.
They all came to live together in one miserable little house. The house
proved to be just too miserable and they decided to go away and find
a better place to live.
   As they set out upon the road the man stumbled over some objects.

He picked them up and felt them. He knew what they were, counted them and exclaimed, "They are seven *eyes!*"

He immediately gave two eyes to himself, two eyes to his wife and one eye each to his mother and his mother-in-law. He still had one eye left. What was he to do? His mother was looking at him hopefully with one eye. His mother-in-law was looking at him hopefully with one eye. To whom should he give the leftover eye?

If he gave the eye to his own mother how can he face his sweet wife? If he gave the eye to his mother-in-law, he must listen to the complaining of his sharp-tongued mother. He began to wonder if life was not better before he found the eyes?

If this problem came to you, what would you do?

Story Notes

This story is adapted from "The Leftover Eye" in *Yes and No: The Intimate Folklore of Africa* by Alta Jablow (Horizon Press, 1961). I use this story only in selected situations with adolescents and older. It is a story that has to be given time to take on meaning, and, facilitating the discussion that is a part of it also requires some experience in working with group processes.

From time to time, I am asked to present to groups of gifted and talented students and/or train their teachers. This is a story I include because it requires the listener to bring a compassionate heart as well as a quick wit—an aspect sometimes overlooked in special programs for bright youngsters. It is not possible to discuss this story without bringing up the needs of the different characters. To do that effectively the listeners have to play out the consequences of each character having and not having the leftover eye.

Story Formula

Blind man has blind mother, blind wife, blind mother-in-law.

They leave too-small house seeking better place.

On the journey man finds seven eyes, gives his wife and himself two each, his mother and mother-in-law one each. Who gets leftover eye?

WHO IS THE MIGHTIEST?

The king orders the thief captured and put in prison.
The king is the mightiest.

The thief shoots the king's tiger.
The thief is also mighty.

The tiger eats the deer.
The tiger is also mighty.

The deer devours the grasslands, causing a famine.
The king dies of hunger.
The deer is also mighty.

Who is the mightiest?

Story Notes

This story is a good example of brevity combined with complexity. I like this story for many reasons, but probably the strongest reason is that there are so few stories which make clear the interdependence of all created beings—"Otter's Revenge" (p. 52) is another. This tale is adapted from a story by the same name in *I Saw a Rocket Walk a Mile: Nonsense Tales, Chants and Songs From Many Lands*.

This story works best with older children and adults in a small group setting. There are several ways to tell the story; one way might be to simply tell and then discuss it, another way might be to use a story board (flannel board, overhead projector, chalk talk). The visuals will help in exploring meaning with your group.

Story Formula

King puts thief in prison.
Thief shoots king's tiger.
Tiger eats deer.
Deer eats the grasslands causing famine.
All die, including King.
Who is mightiest?

THE YOUNG WOMAN AND THE KING'S TASKS

Once there was a King who was riding through his kingdom when he saw a young woman sitting by a window. She was quite beautiful and he fell in love with her at once but did not speak to her. Returning to his castle he began to think only of her. Finally, he decided that he would ask her to marry him. The King wanted to ask her to marry him but he hesitated. Before his death, the young King's father had made him promise to choose only the cleverest wife to rule with him so that the kingdom would prosper. All the women he had met since were often beautiful but usually of average intelligence. He wanted to be sure this young woman was as clever as she was beautiful. He made a plan.

He sent a messenger to the young woman saying that the King desired her company but she must come with and without a present, both riding and walking. The young woman was pleased to be asked to visit the King as she had seen him on that same day when she was sitting by the window, and she too thought only of him. All through the night she wrestled with the problem. By morning's light she was ready.

Interrupt the story at this point and ask your listeners to make some guesses as to how to solve the problem . . . When enough discussion has transpired, resume by saying, "Let's see what the story says."

She borrowed a small donkey from a neighbor, a bird cage from another, and snared a dove from the dovecote.

Stop again and ask if the audience can figure what she will do with these items. Then resume by saying, "Let's see what the story says."

The young woman came to the castle gate with one leg carried on the donkey and one leg walking. In the birdcage was the dove. She called for the King to come out and greet her. He came smiling at the sight of her.

"Behold, your majesty, I come both riding and walking. As for the gift that is not a gift, hold out your hand."

The King did as he was told. The young woman reached in the birdcage and gently took the dove and offered it to the King. When the King reached for the bird, the young woman opened her hand and it flew away.

The King knew he had found the one who should rule with him and they were married soon after.

Story Notes

This story is my weaving together of a well-known set of motifs (H1053–1056) involving paradoxical feats, such as walking and riding with a gift that is not a gift. Folk literature is full of such feats; sometimes several occur in the same story. A few more examples are: neither full nor hungry, in sun or in shadow, clothed or naked. These are wonderful stories with which to challenge children.

Story Formula

King must marry cleverest woman, falls in love, sets young woman tasks: come riding and walking, with and without a present.

She comes one leg on and one leg off donkey, with a dove which she releases when offered to King.

Other Stories

Stories with Similar Motifs:

"With and Without" from *Noodles, Nitwits and Numskulls* by Maria Leach, p. 103 (Dell Publishing, 1961).

"The Mastermaid" (Norwegian) from *World Tales* by Idris Shah, p. 46 (Harcourt, Brace, Jovanovich, 1979). A tender story of a maid winning a king then losing his love through treachery. Her cleverness and love win him back.

CHAPTER 10

Don't Count Your Chickens Before They're Hatched

The "Air Castles" Story

If wishes were horses, then beggars could ride.
—Nursery Rhyme

Have you ever bought something with money you did not yet have, or planned for something that didn't come to pass? If so, then you will recognize the very human theme of the "air castle" story. It is a type which frequently appears in folk literature. More than most formula tales this type is cautionary, that is, it has an obvious, though unspoken, moral.

The moral is defined by Stith Thompson as, "lack of foresight destroys profit." However, Idris Shah, in the notes on his story, "Don't Count Your Chickens," points out: "Emphases of the meaning vary. With the Brahmin, it is greed and lack of foresight, with the Persian devotee in the Turkish, it is undue concentration on one thing; in the Arabian *Kalila* and elsewhere, there is a hint that violent action is it's own undoing" (p. 18).

This type of story is enjoyable for all audiences because most all recognize themselves in it and can have a gentle laugh at themselves from the distance of the story.

THE PAIL OF MILK

Once there was a milkmaid who hired herself out to a farmer to help with his cows. The farmer paid her with a large pail of milk. Elena balanced the pail on her head and started towards home. As she walked, she began to think of what she would do with her milk.

"I will take the milk to market to sell and with that money buy eight eggs which I will put under my best laying hen. She'll hatch me eight chickens, which I will feed with rich grain and they will lay lots of eggs, which I can sell." Elena grew excited thinking of her good luck.

"And with the money I will buy a pig. I will feed that pig with barley and acorns until he is so big and fat he can hardly walk. Then, when fair day comes, I will sell the pig for a good price and with that money I will buy a milk cow that will give me many pails of milk." She began to shout. "I will be able to sell milk from my very own cows! I will become so rich that the handsomest young men will ask me to dance at festival time."

Elena began to twirl and dance about when—*oops*—the pail fell and spilled all over the ground along with all her dreams. Elena sat in the road thinking of her lost fortune:

"Good-bye milk, good-bye eggs, good-bye chickens, good-bye pig, good-bye cow and good-bye handsome young men."

And to you I say, "Good-bye."

Story Notes

"The Pail of Milk," my version of Motif J2061.1: *Air castle,* is drawn from several readings of this particular twist on the familiar story as well as a telling by puppeteer Shari Lewis on her television show, *Shari and Friends.* Since it is short, lighthearted, and leaves the listener with a sense of closure, it makes an excellent ending for a program. The good-bye to the audience allows for a smooth transition to the end of the program.

Story Formula

Farm girl dreams of riches from sale of pail of milk which will buy
    eggs, which will produce chickens who will give more eggs to
    sell.
With money she will buy a pig which she will sell for a cow which

will produce milk which will make her rich and all the young men will want to dance with her.

She twirls and dances about thus spilling milk.

THE DAYDREAMER

Once a poor man walking in the woods happened to find a fox asleep in the sun. The man crouched behind a bush waiting for the right moment to snare the fox. As he waited, he began to dream of what he would do with the fox pelt after he had caught and skinned it.

"I will buy a sow who is about to have piglets. She will deliver at least twelve piglets and those piglets will have piglets. Then I will butcher them and have a whole barn full of meat. I will sell that and have money enough to buy land and marry a fine lady. She will bear me two sons, Peter and James. The boys will plow the field and I will sit by the window and give orders. And, because they will have grown up never knowing poverty as I have, I will have to yell after them, 'Hey, you get going!'" He said these words so loud that he woke up the fox who ran away, taking his skin with him—yes and the pigs, the fine lady, the riches, and the two sons, too.

Story Notes

"The Daydreamer" varies from "The Pail of Milk" only in the details of the daydream, but I include this second "air castles" story here to give you an idea of the range of variants there are. *The Storyteller's Sourcebook* cites a number of other possibilities that initiate the dream of wealth: a jar of honey, basket of glassware, hide of a sleeping deer, jar of barley meal (p. 243). In another variant cited, two hunters argue over how they shall prepare the geese they are aiming at. They argue so loudly that the geese fly away.

Story Formula

Poor man sees sleeping fox and dreams of selling pelt for pregnant
  sow.

Its piglets when grown, he will sell for meat.
Money from meat will make him rich.
He will marry and have two sons.
Sons will be lazy and he will have to shout, "Hey, you get going!"
Startles fox, who runs off.

THE BAG OF RICE

Once there was a man so lazy he refused all work. He would beg in the market place. One day a rich man took pity on him and gave him a bag of rice. The man took the bag home, poured it into his rice pot and lay down on his mat.

"I have done all the work I will do today."

As he lay back, he began to think aloud.

"When the rice crop fails, as it must sometime, and the cost of rice is high, I will sell my rice and buy a cow and a bull. They will give me many calves which I will sell when they are grown. In no time at all I will become rich and marry a strong, hard working woman who will bear me a child which I will take care of while she works in the fields.

"Of course she will probably not want to do all the work herself and we will argue. 'No, I won't,' she will say, and I will say, 'Yes, you will' and kick her out of the house."

With that last thought he kicked his foot and knocked over the pot of rice. The rice spilled everywhere and a neighbor's pigs came in and ate all of it, and the lazy man had nothing left but his broken pot.

Story Notes

This story is based on a tale from Laos (Maguire, p. 53). I include it because it has a different emphasis than "The Pail of Milk" and "The Daydreamer." In the first two, the main character is honest and hard working, but falls victim to his or her own overactive imagination. "The Bag of Rice" portrays the rewards of laziness and uses the "air castles" device to accomplish it.

When telling, be aware that there is an interior monologue going on, as in "The Pail of Milk," and that you are letting your audience in on the talk. Practice it as if it were a conversation with yourself. That is, you will be looking at your audience when you are narrating and over their heads when you are monologuing.

Story Formula

Poor man is too lazy to work.

Rich man gives him a bag of rice.

Man dreams of selling rice to buy a bull and a cow to get a herd and thereby get a wife and child.

Wife will do all the work while he tends child.

She will object and he'll have to kick her out of the house.

He kicks over pail of rice.

Other Stories

Other "Air Castles" Stories

"The Wise Men of Gotham" from *More English Folk and Fairy Tales* by Joseph Jacobs, p. 222 (Putnam, n.d.). Two men argue over which way the sheep, not yet bought, will return home.

"Josefina" from *Word Weaving: A Guide to Storytelling* by Catherine Farrell, p. 59 Word Weaving, Inc., 1987, (Word Weaving, P.O. Box 5646, San Francisco, CA 94101). A delightful Mexican version that includes the Spanish words for eggs, chicken, etc. A good story for teaching about Spanish culture.

"The Milkmaid and Her Bucket" from *Famous Fables for Little Troupers*, by Greta Lipson, p. 126 (Good Apple, 1984). This version of the "air castles" type is based on Aesop's fable "The Girl and the Pitcher of Milk." Lipson's book adapts several fables for creative drama by children in grades K-6. This would be a good story to learn for group participation and Lipson's book would be helpful in structuring children's parts.

"Don't Count Your Chickens" from *World Tales* by Idris Shah, p. 18 (Harcourt, Brace, Jovanovich, 1979). Shah gives a Spanish version of the tale in which the woman dreams of wealth and marriage, even to the point of imagining her sons and daughters-in-law.

CHAPTER 11

It's All in How You Look at It

The Good/Bad Story

> *The web of our life is a mingled yarn, good and ill together.*
> —William Shakespeare, *All's Well that Ends Well*

In every folktale there is always some gritty folk wisdom underlying the story's action. The good/bad story is no exception. This story type sets up contradictory statements in a conversational form and calls them alternately "good" or "bad," by either the audience joining in or by the second voice in the story. Each time the response comes "that's good" or "that's bad," it takes the listener to the next set in the chain which is worse than the last.

This type of story is known to folklorists as "the climax of horrors." Thompson points out that there are not many variants of this type and it is not generally found beyond English speaking peoples (p. 234). I have found this story type repeated, with details varying, in many a storyteller's repertoire. THE FOLKTELLERS, two storytellers named Barbara Freeman and Connie Regan-Black, who work in tandem, have made their very funny Southern version of "News!" quite well-known at storytelling festivals.

NEWS!

A man returns home after being gone a long time and he asks his servant how he managed in his absence.

Owner: Hello, how are things at home?

Servant: None too good. Your old dog, Magpie, died.

Owner: That's too bad, he was a favorite of mine. Did he die of old age?
Servant: Not at all. He overate.

Owner: Good grief, what did he eat so much of?
Servant: Horseflesh, he died of eating horseflesh.

Owner: Horseflesh, where on earth would he get enough horseflesh to gorge himself on?
Servant: Well, all your horses are dead, sir.

Owner: All my horses dead! How did they all die?
Servant: Overwork, sir.

Owner: How were they overworked?
Servant: Carrying water. Yessir, carrying water.

Owner: And why did they have to carry water?
Servant: To put out the fire.

Owner: What fire!!
Servant: Your father's house, next door, burned down.

Owner: Oh, my word, How did the fire get started?
Servant: Everyone thinks it was probably the candles.

Owner: The candles, what candles?
Servant: At your mother's funeral.

Owner: My mother's dead?
Servant: Sorry to say it's true. Everyone says she died of grief.

Owner: Died of grief. Why, what happened?
Servant: Well sir, the truth is your father died since you left.

Owner: My father's gone, too?
Servant: Yessir, some say the shock was too much for him.

Owner: The shock?
Servant: Yes, your poor father was taken ill when word got to him.

Owner: What, more bad news?
Servant: Yessir, your business has failed and your money's all lost. As I knew you would want to know, I made it my business to tell you.

Story Notes

This story is one of the original "climax of horrors" stories (Motif Z23.1, Type 2014) Thompson refers to as a chain having a more literary quality and it may not have originated in the oral tradition (p. 234). My retelling is adapted from the classic version by the same name (Jacobs, *More* . . . p. 182). When I tell this story I do not memorize word-for-word but use a more conversational tone, as though I were telling a humorous anecdote; hence it varies a great deal in length and detail each time I tell it.

Story Formula

Owner returns after a long absence and hears that:
dog has died from overeating because
ate too much horseflesh because
there was an excess of dead horses because
horses were all overworked hauling water for fire because
owners father's house burned down because
of candles from funeral of mother because
she died of grief because
father died of shock because
owner's business and fortune failed.

Other Stories

Other Version:

"Good and Bad News" (Norwegian) reprinted in *Best Loved Folktales of the World* selected by Joanna Cole, p. 212 (Doubleday, 1983). This version has the bad news of marrying a "shrew" and the good news that "she died in the fire." While I don't like stories hostile to women or men, this one is worth reading to appreciate differences in the story type.

GOOD OR BAD?

There was this pilot who went up in an airplane whose engine had just been repaired.
    That's good.
No, that's bad. The engine didn't work that day.
    Oh, that's bad.
No, that's good. The pilot had a parachute.
    That's good.
No, that's bad. The parachute didn't open.
    That's bad.
No, that's good. There was a haystack under him when he landed.
    That's good.
No, that's bad. There was a pitchfork in the haystack.
    That's bad.
No, that's good. He missed the pitchfork.
    That's good.
No, that's bad. He missed the haystack, too.

Story Notes

This is a well-known chain story that is from American folk literature and fits the "Climax of Horrors" motif (Z23.1; Type 2014). I first heard this from a sixth grade teacher who demonstrated with his class. I have since added a few of my own refinements. Word-for-word memorization is not necessary, but you will want to stick fairly closely to the text.

Other Stories

Other Versions:

"Good or Bad" from *I Saw a Rocket Walk a Mile: Nonsense Tales, Chants and Songs From Many Lands* by Carl Withers, p. 32 (Holt, Rinehart and Winston, 1965).
"Ike and Mike" from *Creative Storytelling* by Jack Maguire, p. 53 (McGraw-Hill, 1985).

WHO'S TO SAY IT'S BAD LUCK?

Once there was a farmer who had a large herd of horses that had run away because the gate had been left open.

"That's bad luck," said a neighboring farmer who was passing by.

"Who's to say it's bad luck?" shrugged the farmer.

Several evenings later all the horses returned on their own to the corral and among the herd was a magnificent wild stallion.

The neighboring farmer saw the beautiful animal and said, "What good luck! You have a fine stallion to add to your herd."

"Who's to say it's good luck?" the farmer shrugged.

The next day the farmer's son decided to tame the stallion. He roped it and jumped on its back. Immediately, the strong horse bucked and the son fell off, breaking his leg. The neighboring farmer heard the news and came to visit. He shook his head at the poor young man who had to remain in bed. "What bad luck that your son has broken his leg. Now you have no one to help you."

"Who's to say it's bad luck?" shrugged the farmer.

A few days later soldiers came into the area conscripting all able bodied young men into the King's army. The farmer's son was not taken because of his broken leg. All the other farmer's sons were sent to foreign lands and none returned.

The farmer rejoiced in both his good luck and his bad luck.

Story Notes

This story is based on a version I read a number of years ago in *Living Positively One Day at a Time* by Dr. Robert Schuller (Jove Pubns., 1986). It is a variation on the good/bad story type and its main focus is not to entertain but to provoke thought. This story has the feel of the Buddhist teaching tales, wherein some aspect of human nature is neatly and briefly presented for contemplation. In this instance the story demonstrates that it is our perception of human events which controls how we will feel about them.

This story could be used in many settings, as even elementary age children would derive some benefit from this story. However, the very best hearing will be with older children and adults. Since it is really a moral tale, it could be used as an introduction in a program or meeting of any kind in which you wish to make a point about perceptions, or seeing things in a different light.

Story Formula

Farmer loses herd through open gate
Bad luck?
Herd returns with a wild stallion
Good luck?
Son tries to tame stallion and breaks his leg
Bad luck?
King conscripts all able-bodied men. Son cannot go. All soldiers killed.
Farmer rejoices in good luck and bad luck.

BIBLIOGRAPHY

Afanas'ev, Aleksandr. *Russian Fairy Tales.* New York: Pantheon Books, 1945.

Ausubel, Nathan, ed. *A Treasury of Jewish Folklore.* New York: Crown, 1948.

Aarne, Antti and Stith Thompson. *The Types of the Folktale: A Classification and Bibliography.* Folklore Fellows Communications, no. 184. Helsinki: Suomalainen Tiedeakatemia, 1961.

Barton, Bob. *Tell Me Another.* Ontario: Pembroke, 1986.

Briggs, Katharine M. *A Dictionary of British Folk-tales in the English Language.* Bloomington: University of Indiana Press, 1970.

Brunvand, Jan. *The Study of American Folklore: An Introduction.* New York: W. W. Norton, 1968.

Clarkson, Atelia and Gilbert Cross. *World Folktales: A Scribner Resource Collection.* New York: Macmillan, 1982.

Cole, Joanna, ed. *Best Loved Folktales of the World.* New York: Doubleday, 1983.

Courlander, Harold and Wolf Leslan. *The Fire on the Mountain and Other Ethiopian Tales.* New York: Holt, Rinehart and Winston, 1956.

Dailey, Sheila. *Storytelling: A Creative Teaching Strategy.* Mt. Pleasant, Michigan: Storytime Productions, 1985. (1326 E. Broadway Mt. Pleasant, MI 48858).

DeSpain, Pleasant. *Twenty-two Splendid Tales to Tell.* Little Rock: August House, 1994.

Farrell, Catherine. *Word Weaving: A Guide to Storytelling.* San Francisco: Word Weaving, 1987. (P.O. Box 5646 San Francisco, CA 94101).

Grimm, Jacob and Wilhelm. *The Complete Grimm's Fairy Tales.* New York: Pantheon, 1944.

Haviland, Virginia, ed. *The Fairy Tale Treasury.* New York: Dell Publishing, 1972.

Jacobs, Joseph. *English Fairy Tales.* New York: Penguin, 1971.

———. *More English Folk and Fairy Tales,* New York: Putnam, n.d.

Lewis, C. S. "Of Other Worlds" in *On Stories.* New York: Harcourt, Brace, Jovanovich, 1966.

Livo, Norma J. and Sandra A. Reitz. *Storytelling: Process and Practice.* Littleton, Co.: Libraries Unlimited, 1986.

———. *Storytelling Folklore Sourcebook.* Littleton, Co.: Libraries Unlimited, 1991.

Luthi, Max. *Once Upon A Time: On the Nature of Fairy Tales.* Bloomington: Indiana University Press, 1970.

Maguire, Jack. *Creative Storytelling.* New York: McGraw-Hill, 1985.

MacDonald, Margaret Read. *The Storyteller's Sourcebook: A Subject, Title and Motif Index to Folklore Collections for Children.* Detroit: Neal-Schuman/Gale Research, 1982.

Moran, Barbara. "The Number Three in Fairy Tales and Folklore." *The National Storytelling Journal,* Vol. IV, No. 1. (Winter 1989).

Papashvily, George and Helen. *Yes and No Stories: A Book of Georgian Folk Tales.* New York: Harper and Row, 1946.

Opie, Iona and Peter. *The Classic Fairy Tales.* London: Oxford University Press, 1980.

Ross, Ramon. *Storyteller.* New York: Charles E. Merrill, 1980.

Sawyer, Ruth. *The Way of the Storyteller.* New York: Viking, 1942.

Schwartz, Alvin. *Scary Stories to Tell in the Dark.* New York: J. B. Lippincott, 1981.

Shah, Idris. *World Tales.* New York: Harcourt, Brace, Jovanovich, 1979.

Shannon, George. *Stories to Solve: Folktales from Around the World.* New York: Greenwillow, 1985.

Shedlock, Marie L. *The Art of the Storyteller.* New York: Dover, 1951. (First pub. 1915.)

Thompson, Stith. *Motif-Index of Folk-Literature.* Bloomington and London: Indiana University Press, 1966. 6 vols.

———. *The Folktale.* Fort Worth, Tx.: Dryden Press, 1946.

Withers, Carl. *I Saw a Rocket Walk a Mile: Nonsense Tales, Chants and Songs From Many Lands.* New York: Holt, Rinehart and Winston, 1965.

Zall, P. M., ed. *A Hundred Merry Tales and Other English Jest Books from the Fifteenth and Sixteenth Century.* Lincoln: Univ. of Nebraska Pr., 1963.